THRESHOLD TO
GOD'S WORD

A user-friendly guide
to Scripture study

STEPHEN J. BINZ

TWENTY
THIRD 23rd
PUBLICATIONS
www.23rdpublications.com

TWENTY-THIRD PUBLICATIONS

1 Montauk Avenue, Suite 200, New London, CT 06320

(860) 437-3012 » (800) 321-0411 » www.23rdpublications.com

ISBN: 978-1-62785-028-5

Library of Congress Catalog Card Number: 2014935252

Printed in the U.S.A.

Contents

❖ ❖ ❖

Preface · vii

1] Opening the Door to Christ · · · · · · · · · · · · · · · 1

2] The Threshold of Christian Discipleship · · · · 14

Crossing the Threshold....

3] From Paper and Ink to the Living
Word of God · 27

4] From Bondage and Death to Freedom
and Life · 39

5] From Creation to New Creation · · · · · · · · · · · · 52

6] From Literalism to Fuller Meaning · · · · · · · · 66

7] From Information to Transformation · · · · · · · 80

8] From Distraction to Deep Listening · · · · · · · · 92

9] From Listening to Responding in Prayer · · 107

10] From Word to Worship to Witness · · · · · · · 119

Endnotes · 132

Preface

A few years ago, when I first began writing the Threshold Bible Study series, I was in the midst of what many call the midlife transition. It was a period of life when I was leaving behind the first half of life and moving into the second half, yet with great uncertainty about what it would bring. It was a time of anxiety, insecurity about the future, and lack of confidence in the direction my life should take.

I chose the image of the threshold because I came to realize that everyone experiences these transitions at different periods of life, these pauses at the threshold before experiencing something new. As I continued to move through this midlife transition, the threshold became a powerful symbol for me of the spiritual journey, of invitation to growth, and of richer life in Christ. Gradually, through placing myself in new experiences and facing new challenges, I crossed the threshold into the second half of life. And looking back across that threshold, I now discovered myself in a much better place, a place enriched by the wisdom of experience, the confidence of inner peace, a joy in my life's mission, and a deep love for Christ, his church, the Scriptures, and the gift of my discipleship.

Writing the various thematic books in the Threshold Bible
Study series has helped me to focus on my own spiritual growth
and to realize my contribution to the growth of others who
read them. The series of symbols and images that form the
themes of these books—the cross, the divine heart, Eucharist,
the light of Advent, gifts of the Spirit, the names of Jesus, angels, resurrection, Jerusalem, the Earth, pilgrimage, and many
more—have led me into a fuller life with God. Each theme has
been an opportunity to discover a different aspect of God's
word. Reflecting on Scripture and writing this series has been
healing and life-giving. It has helped me understand myself, my
faith, and the mission and ministry I have been given.

I hope that this book and the Threshold series will be equal-
ly enriching and life-giving for you. Opening the door to Christ,
crossing the threshold, and entering a fuller life is God's desire
for each of us. And, as you will see in this book, the experience
of encountering Christ in Scripture is like crossing a threshold,
moving us to fuller peace, purpose, and possibility.

The best compliment I can receive after giving a talk or
writing a book is this: "You opened some important new doors
for me." God continually prepares our lives to be renewed, and
various people, experiences, and insights help us cross over to
something new. I hope that this book provides that entryway
for you, a door that you can open and enter into a new experience of God's word.

One of the people for whom I am immensely grateful is the
spiritual writer Joyce Rupp. Her book *Dear Heart, Come Home:
The Path of Midlife Spirituality* offered me insights to manage
the midlife transition. And her later book, *Open the Door: A
Journey to the True Self*, helped me reflect on the image of the
threshold in more personal and spiritual ways.

This book may be used by individual readers to gain a better understanding of Scripture or by a community reading and

discussing together. It is ideal for groups who are using or preparing to use Threshold Bible Study. This book may be used to invite people to experience Bible study and to deepen the experience of those already studying Scripture on their own or with others.

The end of each chapter contains a list of "Keys for Unlocking the Door," a series of "Questions for Reflection at the Threshold," and finally a "Prayer for Crossing the Threshold." These are only prompts that encourage the reader to continue to reflect and pray about the contents of each chapter.

These keys, questions, and prayers will be helpful both to individual readers and to groups. A group may study this book by reading a chapter each week on their own and then gathering together to discuss the keys and the questions, and then concluding with the prayer. In this way, group members will benefit from the insights of one another and encourage each other in their ongoing study of Scripture.

This book is an encouragement to respond to the invitation of Jesus Christ at the threshold. It is the beginning of a journey of exploration and discovery that lasts a lifetime. I pray that the encouragement provided in this book will move you to make reflective reading of Scripture a more regular and central part of your life as a Christian disciple.

STEPHEN J. BINZ

1 Opening the Door to Christ

THE BOOK OF REVELATION PRESENTS US WITH A MARVEL-OUS IMAGE OF JESUS CHRIST. It is an invitation to open the door and let him in. He is standing outside, knocking, seeking entrance.

> *"Listen! I am standing at the door, knocking; if you hear my voice and open the door, I will come into you and eat with you, and you with me."* [REV 3:20]

The divine guest is waiting at the door. He does not force his entry. He knocks and waits with patience for each of us to open the door of our life to him. His voice speaks the word of God to us, beckoning us to hear the good news that he offers. If we open the door and let him cross over the threshold, he will nourish and enrich our lives.

The risen Jesus is present in his church, in the Scriptures, in the world around us, and in people we encounter. Yet to invite him into our lives requires awareness of his knocking and attentiveness to his voice. He tells us first that we must "listen." Too often our lives are too noisy and too busy to be aware and attentive to his invitation. Any time that we can slow down our lives, stop and reflect on their meaning, be silent and think about the direction we are moving, or pause for an open and trustful conversation with a friend, we are preparing ourselves to open the door.

Jesus says that those who open the door and welcome him into their lives will eat with him. Eating and drinking in the presence of God is a frequent biblical metaphor for communion of life. Sharing in the divine life is like sharing in a banquet, "a feast of rich food, a feast of well-matured wines," as Isaiah describes it (Isa 25:6). For Christians, this nourishment is received most fully in the word and sacrament of Eucharist. "I will come into you," Jesus says, "and eat with you, and you with me." He offers us a communion that is both nourishing and transforming.

Opening the door to Christ requires a decision. It means making a concerted effort to unlock the bolt, to welcome him across the threshold, to open our heart to his presence, to listen to his voice, to receptively invite the good news into our lives, and to receive the fullness of life that he offers.

Inviting Christ across the Threshold

Each of us, since we are made in the image of God, is a vast treasure house. Although we could spend a lifetime of exploration, none of us will ever discover all the wonders that are inside of us. Saint Paul describes the human person as a temple. "Do you not know," he writes, "that you are God's temple and that God's Spirit dwells in you?" (1 Cor 3:16). As we invite Jesus across the threshold, we can explore the richness that God has placed within us and share in divine life.

As creatures made by God, created in the divine image, we

have a natural desire for God. There is within us a restlessness and longing for God until that desire for God is satisfied. As a temple created for God to dwell within, our deepest heart's desire is for God to live in us. For this reason, we must realize that Christ is at the door, knocking and speaking to us, beckoning us to open the door and let him in.

When we let Christ cross over the threshold, he leads us to explore the many rooms and dwelling places within ourselves. When we open doors in our interior being, we discover our own spiritual wealth. Exploring our inner dwelling places, we find wisdom we did not know we had, strength we were unaware of, goodness we have never expressed, and undiscovered gifts that we can use in service.

Because we spend most of our awake hours focusing on our external life, we spend little time or energy on our interior life. What if we regularly made time to explore our inner reality? God's temple within us is always open to us if we are willing to be still and attentive long enough to visit it. Christ is waiting at the door, ready to be let in, to lead our discovery, to speak to us and guide our journey.

After we welcome our divine guest across the threshold, he leads us to explore some places within ourselves that we would rather ignore. Areas of pain and grief are hidden within us; anger and criticism are around the corner; selfishness and apathy have their places of residence. All of these dark and unexplored rooms are waiting for the light of Christ's presence and for his healing touch. Every moment is open to possibilities of God's revelation. On our interior journey, we pass through many rooms that can deepen our self-knowledge and open us to trust God's Spirit dwelling within the temple.

When we welcome Jesus Christ across the threshold of our lives, we open ourselves to change in ways we may have never dreamed likely. We open our lives to transformation. The One through whom we were made can enable us to become more fully our authentic selves, the persons we were created to be. Following his lead and listening to his voice, we are able to move into our own sacred space, our inner sanctuary, where we discover our heart, the source of our deepest desire.

Standing at the Threshold

A threshold can be described as a state of transition—the movement from the secure to the unknown, from the routine to the surprise, from a narrow viewpoint to a wider vision. The threshold always offers opportunities for personal transformation, and indeed it is at the threshold that most of the real learning in life occurs.

There are moments in life when a door opens in our consciousness to make something clearer than it was before, leading us from a previous way of understanding to a new way of seeing life. Sometimes an external event creates this threshold opportunity. At other times it is established by more of an internal shift, a graced moment for which we can only be grateful.

Sometimes the door opens for just a moment, sometimes forever. These threshold opportunities can be short-lived, or they can be life-changing. The quality of the experience depends on what we do at the threshold. Whether or not personal change and transformation occurs depends on whether or not we accept and welcome the opportunity at the threshold.

Anthropologists and psychologists explore these threshold states, often called "liminal" states, from the Latin word for threshold, which is *limen*. Rites of passages are often described as liminal experiences, leading from one stage of life to another, enabling new perspectives. Jungian psychologists describe self-realization as a movement through liminal space and time, from disorientation to integration. The difficult phase of liminality serves the purpose of making a person whole, giving one a deeper sense of meaning, purpose, and relatedness.

The Catholic Church uses this terminology to refer to the periodic *ad limina* visit to Rome required of every bishop, literally to the threshold of the apostles, Peter and Paul, to pray at their tombs as a sign of unity and apostolicity. The author Richard Rohr writes about suffering as a liminal experience—those painful life experiences when we are not in control, in which our ego can be transcended and we can learn something genuinely new and life-changing.

The threshold opportunity is a sacred space and a graced time. In the Bible, Jacob experienced a threshold moment in his dream, in which he encountered God between heaven and earth. In that fearful encounter, Jacob received a new understanding of his life in relationship to God (Gen 28:12–19). Isaiah received his threshold opportunity in the temple of Jerusalem, in which he experienced God's ineffable holiness and accepted the call to be sent by God as a prophet (Isa 6:1–8). Jonah experienced his liminal time in the belly of the great fish. Fearful and out of control, Jonah could only pray and surrender to God's will for him to go to Nineveh.

The threshold is often an uncomfortable place, full of fear, a time of testing. Jesus experienced such a time when he was driven into the wilderness before his public ministry. Reflecting on the book of Deuteronomy and tempted by demonic powers, he grew to better understand his divine mission and submitted his life to the Father's will. The season of Lent should be a threshold experience for catechumens and all believers—a period of spiritual disciplines, of fasting and prayer, a transition and time of growth—leading to a new and deeper experience of the paschal mystery.

In order to see the doorway and experience the threshold opportunity, we need to break out of our routine patterns that keep our lives predictable and secure. Experiences like retreats, periods of fasting, and pilgrimages can break us out of the ordinary, present us with occasions of discomfort or disorientation, and open to us the threshold. Worship can lead us corporately into the threshold moment. Through ritual, Scripture, prayer, music, and sacrifice, we are brought to the threshold experience, and then sent back transformed into the world to serve.

Bible Study at the Threshold

The study of Scripture can be a threshold opportunity when we truly encounter God in the sacred texts. This is accomplished not by ordinary reading, but through reading Scripture as the word of God. This kind of reflective reading requires a deep listening and confidence that God has placed his own Spirit in the inspired texts. When the Scriptures are read with this intention and expectation, the biblical page can become a threshold, a place where we can truly meet our God.

In Paul's first letter to the Thessalonians, he expressed gratitude to God for his readers because they accepted the good news of Jesus Christ not as a "human word" but rather as "God's word."

> We constantly give thanks to God for this, that when
> you received the word of God that you heard from
> us, you accepted it not as a human word but as what
> it really is, God's word, which is also at work in you
> believers. {1 THES 2:13}

Paul makes it clear that the gospel he proclaims is not his own thoughts or an interesting piece of human wisdom. Paul considered himself and his missionary companions only as instruments to preach and spread God's word. Once this word has been communicated by Paul to his hearers, the divine word has its own power to enter into the lives of those who accept it. When the word of God is welcomed into the lives of believers, it is "at work" within them, transforming their lives with the message of salvation. This reception of the believer, which is faith, is the key that opens the door to God's word.

What gives meaning to the world and purpose to the lives of Christian believers is the word of God. God has spoken the divine word in the history of salvation and revealed the divine self to us. In the face of everything else in which we are tempted to place our hopes—like material possessions, physical pleasures, and worldly power—the word of God is eternal. As the prophet Isaiah proclaimed, "The grass withers, the flower fades, but the word of our God will stand forever" (Isa 40:8). While all else withers and fades, proving to be momentary and fleeting, God's word endures forever.

This divine self-communication, God's eternal word, is expressed definitively in the life, death, and resurrection of Jesus Christ. In his first letter, Peter echoes and expands the words of Isaiah: "The word of the Lord endures forever. That word is the good news that was announced to you" (1 Pet 1:25). This word of God has been entrusted to the church, which then hands it on through the apostles and its apostolic tradition. The mission of the church is to proclaim the word of God to the world.

This understanding that Scripture is God's self-revelation and divinely inspired means that we hear, read, experience, and share it with others as the word of God. When we carefully listen to this word, reflect on its message, and respond in faith to God's presence there, we truly encounter God in the sacred text. This is how believers have read the Scriptures through the ages. Although we can read the biblical books as merely a human word, as a collection of ancient literature, when we read these texts as the word of God, we can truly encounter our God there and be transformed in that encounter.

Reading the Bible as the Book of Christ

God communicates divine truth, love, desire for unity with humankind, and indeed God's very self through the Bible. The good news found in Scripture is called the word of God because it is God's self-revelation to us. At the same time, Jesus himself is called the Word of God because he is the fullest expression of God's self-revelation to humanity. God communicates truth, love, and God's very self through Jesus. Through the powerful work of the Holy Spirit, the Word of God became flesh; and through the inspiration of the Holy Spirit, the word of God became Scripture.

Before Christ came into the world, this word expressed itself in many different ways, multiplied throughout the Scriptures of Israel. God communicated the message of salvation in various and partial ways through the voices of many prophets and inspired writers. But when the fullness of time came, the Word returned to its original unity: "The Word became flesh and lived among us" (John 1:14). Now God speaks to us through Christ:

> Long ago God spoke to our ancestors in many and various ways by the prophets, but in these last days he has spoken to us by a Son, whom he appointed heir of all things. {HEBREWS 1:1–2}

The many words became the one Word, the living Word to which every other word bears witness. God's Word is now not only audible but visible and tangible, now not only spoken but incarnate and living.

Christ, the Word made flesh, has traditionally been called the *Verbum abbreviatum*, the "abbreviated Word." In Christ, the many parts of the Bible are harmonized and unified. John of the Cross put it succinctly in *The Ascent of Mount Carmel*: "In giving us his Son, Who is his only Word, God has said everything to us at once, in one simple stroke, in this single word—and he has nothing more to say."[1]

Evoking the opening words of Scripture, "In the beginning" (Gen 1:1), John's gospel begins its account of God's new creation by stating, "In the beginning was the Word" (John 1:1). John goes on to declare that this Word was "with God" and indeed "the Word was God." And it was through this Word that all things came into being. The divine Word is God's reaching out, seeking to share divine being, sharing eternal love with creation.

God's word began to be known first through creation, then through the Torah and prophets of Israel, and finally through Jesus Christ. As God's self-expression, "the Word" encompasses Jesus' entire ministry, showing that all his words and works flow from his eternal existence and God's self-manifestation in salvation history. As John's prologue proclaims, "The Word became flesh and lived among us" (John 1:14). This incarnation, John shows, is on a scale with the creation of the world. In this new creation, the incarnate Word gives to humanity the power to become children of God, to be reborn, to share intimately in God's life.

The same word of God that became flesh is also given to us through the sacred text of God's people. For this reason, the mystery of Jesus Christ is the center and focus of the whole Christian Bible. He is the key that opens up the full meaning of all parts of Scripture. The Bible is, above all else, the book of Christ.

Jesus himself taught his disciples to see the rich continuity of God's plan of salvation and to appreciate how all of Israel's history pointed to his coming. These teachings came to a climactic moment when the risen Lord appeared to his disciples on the road to Emmaus. Luke tells us, "Then beginning with Moses and all the prophets, he interpreted to them the things about himself in all the scriptures" (Luke 24:27).

For Christians, the death and resurrection of the Lord sheds new light on the Old Testament texts and enriches them with new meaning. Only together do the Old and New Testaments express God's full revelation. As Saint Augustine said, "The New Testament lies hidden in the Old, and the Old Testament is unveiled in the New."[2] We can come to understand the Old Testament fully only when we see it as a mother who bears the New Testament in her womb and gives birth to it.

Of course we can read and interpret the texts of the Old Testament as the literature of Israel and appreciate their value in and of themselves. We can be grateful for these books in their Jewish context and learn from them. Likewise, we can read the New Testament alone, and understand it as the story of Jesus and the early church. But for the Christian believer, the two testaments must be read in light of one another because they form one book in which the mystery of Christ is the focal center.

Because we are believers and because the Holy Spirit works within us, we can see Christ whenever we read a page of sacred Scripture. As Hugh of St. Victor says so beautifully from the twelfth century,

> *All sacred Scripture is but one book, and this one book*
> *is Christ; because all sacred Scripture speaks of Christ,*
> *and all sacred Scripture is fulfilled in Christ.*[3]

In the whole Bible, in all of its parts, we can experience an encounter with God in Christ. Colossians says, "[Christ] is the image of the invisible God, the firstborn of all creation...All things were created through him and for him" (Col 1:15–16). He is the reason for all reality and the destination of history, the Alpha and Omega.

Meditating on Scripture, then, is not so much a matter of interpreting a book as of seeking Someone. It is not primarily an intellectual exercise, but a devoted and passionate search, an enthusiastic and joyful discovery. The meaning we find in Scripture is not impersonal truth but ultimately the person of Jesus Christ.

Welcoming the Word of Life

In Luke's gospel, Jesus tells a parable in which he compares his disciples to servants waiting for their master's return. Jesus teaches his followers to wait for him with expectation, so that they will open the door for him when he knocks.

> *Be like those who are waiting for their master to*
> *return...so that they may open the door for him as soon*
> *as he comes and knocks.* {LUKE 12:36}

When we welcome the word of God into our lives, we open the door for Christ and invite him to cross over the threshold. Because the inspired Scriptures express God's living word, we receive the word of life through our open door, our listening ear, our receptive heart.

When we learn to read the Bible as this kind of invitation, we can expect God to reveal divine presence, marvelous wisdom, and God's sacred way as we study the Scriptures. Reading with this expectation means truly listening, knowing that God's way may be different from our own. It means learning how to read the Bible in a way that doesn't require that we have all the answers, but that requires us to stay present to the text as it makes us present to the divine mystery.

Reading Scripture with this expectation requires us to cultivate a deepening desire for God. Yet, at the same time, we realize that our longing for God is a result of God's deep desire for us. God's grace creates this yearning within us. It is this desire for God that creates the listening ear, the receptive heart, the opening door that is so necessary to hear God's word in Scripture. When we desire God and are ready for this encounter, God's word will invite us into a deeper presence and relationship.

❖ ❖ ❖

KEYS FOR UNLOCKING THE DOOR

Jesus knocks and patiently waits for us to open the door of our lives to him.

Our deepest heart's desire, since we were made by God and for God, is for God to live in us.

The threshold offers a grace-filled opportunity to encounter God.

The biblical text can be a threshold for us when we welcome the word of God with faith.

For Christians, Jesus Christ is the center of Scripture and the key that opens up its full meaning.

The meaning we find in Scripture is not just impersonal or intellectual truth, but ultimately the person of Jesus Christ.

Our desire for God creates the listening ear and the receptive heart that are necessary to hear God's word.

❖ ❖ ❖

QUESTIONS FOR REFLECTION AT THE THRESHOLD

● What kind of door is Christ standing behind? A thick bronze door, a screen door, a transparent etched-glass door, a revolving door...?

- What message have I placed on the doormat? Welcome, do not disturb, mi casa es su casa, wipe your feet, no trespassing, enter at your own risk...?

- How do I hear Christ knocking? Gentle tapping, loud rapping, persistent striking, strong banging, steady knocking...?

- How can I prepare myself to welcome my divine guest?

- What might I discover inside myself if Christ would lead me on an inner journey?

- In what sense is sacred Scripture the one book of Christ?

- What can I do to more deeply and personally experience the Bible as the word of God?

❖ ❖ ❖

PRAYER FOR CROSSING THE THRESHOLD

Lord Jesus, I hear you knocking on the door of my life.
Help me believe in you and deepen my desire for you.
Teach me how to listen, to open my ear and my heart to
the transforming word of God. I welcome you across
the threshold to explore with me the riches of your word,
the potential within me, and the hope that you give to me.

2 The Threshold of Christian Discipleship

WHEN WE LISTEN TO THE VOICE OF JESUS CHRIST AND RE-
SPOND TO HIS KNOCKING ON THE DOOR, WE RECEIVE HIS CALL
TO DISCIPLESHIP. Letting him cross the threshold and enter
into our lives places him in the position of Savior and Lord and
makes us his followers. Allowing him to take the lead acknowl-
edges that he is the Master and Teacher and we are his disciples.

At the beginning of his ministry, Jesus passed along the Sea
of Galilee and said to Peter, Andrew, James, and John, "Follow
me," and they left their nets and followed him. Through their
life with Jesus, the fishermen learned how to live the good news
of God's kingdom and to proclaim it to others.

When Jesus came to Samaria, he approached a woman as
she was drawing water from a well. Although she was surprised
that Jesus would be speaking to her, because she was a Samaritan
and a woman, Jesus led her to the experience of repentance and
enabled her to envision a new future. So the woman left her
water jar, just as the fishermen left their nets, and went to the
Samaritans of her city, proclaimed the good news, and brought
many to Jesus through her testimony about him.

When Jesus was going through Jericho, he encountered the chief tax collector looking down on him from a sycamore tree. When Jesus saw him he insisted, "Zacchaeus, hurry and come down; for I must stay at your house today." When Zacchaeus opened the door to Jesus, he repented of his dishonesty, gave generously to the poor, and his life began to change. As Jesus crossed the threshold and into the life of Zacchaeus, he said, "Today salvation has come to this house."

Jesus continued to call disciples throughout his life, and he continues to call disciples today through the Holy Spirit working in his church. When people hear him knocking and listen to his voice—through the preached word, through the invitation of other disciples, or through the Scriptures—Jesus is calling new disciples. Those who unlock the bolt and open the door of their lives to him receive the offer of salvation and begin to live in his presence.

Discipleship Is God's Gift

A disciple is "one who follows." The disciple walks in the way of Jesus while he leads. The road and the direction are decided by Jesus. At times the way may be broad and pleasant; at other times, narrow and dangerous. Disciples must place great trust in the Master to abandon themselves to his guidance.

The gospels stress the fact that Jesus takes the initiative in discipleship. He invites men and women to "come and follow." In John's gospel, Jesus emphasizes that discipleship is a divine choice: "It was not you who chose me, but I who chose you" (John 15:16). Discipleship is not something that we can earn or that we deserve. It is God's gift. And responding in faith to God's call can only be accepted humbly and with gratitude.

No disciples in the gospels have in themselves the abilities to follow Jesus and to serve the kingdom of God. Even those who became great leaders in the church, like Peter and Paul, knew that their leadership qualities came through their faithful response to Jesus. Through mistakes and failures, they realized that whatever success they offered to the church was due to God's grace.

The fact that new disciples immediately left behind much of their lives to follow Jesus indicates that he must have inspired a great confidence within them. For some of them, what they left behind was a secure living and a predictable life. For others, what they left behind was their brokenness, their sin, and their fears. After becoming a disciple, life is never the same again. The disciple leaves behind anything that impedes the following. Sometimes being a disciple involves emptying one's life of what feels secure, but for the purpose of filling one's life with abundance.

The message proclaimed by Jesus and his early disciples was called "good news," *euangelion*. This is the foundation of Christianity. There is something permanently fresh and urgent about the Christian faith. It is not about abstract principles or generic philosophy. It is news about something unprecedented and astounding. What is this good news? It is essentially this: The long-awaited kingdom of God has come among us in Jesus Christ. Through his life, death, and resurrection, God has forgiven our sins and offered to make us a new creation.

For this reason, the call to discipleship has a "grab you by the lapels" quality about it. The authors of the New Testament are not just writing about a new system of thought or a helpful spirituality. They are telling the world about a revolution. Jesus is risen from the dead and is now universal Lord and King. He is calling all people to be his followers and to transform their whole lives around him through his Spirit and as members of his church.

This is the news that Scripture proclaims. This is the invitation that the Bible offers. This is the gospel that changes hearts and transforms lives. This is the new life that is waiting for every person across the threshold.

Obstacles to God's Word

Sometimes we are unable to welcome Christ across the doorway because of the bolts we have placed on the door. Most often these locks consist of various types of fear. We are afraid of what the Lord will find when we allow him deeply into our lives. We fear the costs of discipleship—the sacrifices it might entail. We are afraid of what we might discover deep within ourselves if we are quiet and make time to listen to God. Maybe we fear that the gospel might just be too good to be true.

Another obstacle we place across the doorway is our refusal to break out of our status-quo lives. The Scriptures assure us that our lives will never be the same again when we welcome Jesus as Lord. Life can no longer be a one-thing-after-another routine. Our priorities will be radically readjusted. The focus of our lives becomes Jesus and the gospel, as we "seek first the kingdom."

Many of our obstacles to God's word are a result of the culture in which we live. An unhealthy secularism creates hostility toward religion and denies the transcendent truths that uplift culture and hold it together. Ultimate human purpose and destiny are beyond the purview of the secular culture. Relativism holds that there is no absolute truth or value. All ideas have only relative, subjective value according to personal differences of opinion. Each individual is ultimately faced with his or her own truth, which is essentially a denial of God, since God is absolute truth. The individualism of our culture maximizes self-interest and loses the traditional sense of the common good. Human life no longer has a purpose that is commonly agreed upon or a conception of the good toward which human life is to aim. And rampant consumerism has perverted our human desires by redirecting them from their natural end in God to an artificial objective in material objects and temporary pleasures.

We live with all the obstacles of our culture, pursuing the four pernicious Ps of power, prestige, pleasure, and possessions, while ignoring the four gracious Gs of God, goodness, grace, and generosity. Yet, in spite of all the obstacles—secularism, relativism, individualism, and consumerism—people still experience a restless discontent and hunger for faith. We desire to fill the empty void created in our hearts with what is truly genuine and lasting, with the lasting nourishment of the gospel. The challenge of Christianity today is how to offer the authentic good news of God's reign to a world staggering under the weight of so many unanswered questions and unfulfilled longings.

Other locks on the door are related to our understanding of the Bible. For example, we think that the Bible is too complex. Yet, in reality, the Bible was never intended to be difficult or contain any mysterious language. It was written by simple and fallible people like ourselves, people who search for God and express God's presence and guidance in their history and their personal lives. The basic questions of people in every age, about human purpose and the meaning of life, are the same questions expressed in the biblical writings. And, while parts of the Bible might seem difficult to understand at first, Bible studies contain commentaries to help readers interpret the meaning of challenging passages.

Another reason we keep a lock on our passageway through the Bible is our view that the Bible is too controversial. Yet the Bible was never intended to cause conflict between people. Using the Bible to prove points or win arguments is an abuse of Scripture. We can leave the controversies to the scholars to hash out. The Bible is the sacred literature of Israel and the church, and we can only approach it in wonder and with humility.

Sometimes we have the false opinion that the Bible is confining. We think it is essentially a collection of commandments, principles, precepts, and ethical lessons designed to correct human behavior. With such a selective focus on laws and regulations, we become convinced that God will embrace us just as soon as we straighten out our lives and become acceptable to him.

But the Bible is not intended to be complex, controversial, or confining. The word of God desires to be captivating. Scripture has offered a deep experience of God's presence to countless people through the ages. When we take away our distorted understandings, God is able to enter our lives with the good news of salvation, to heal us and lead us to the fullness of life.

For all of these reasons, Christian faith is more difficult to cultivate today than it was in past eras. Our reaction to the many obstacles to faith in today's culture might be confusion and withdrawal. These obstructions can cause us to question our identity and the very foundations of our faith. The fact that God is increasingly being driven out of our culture makes it seem that God's revelation in Scripture is locked into an ever more remote past. Yet Christian faith must always be thought out afresh and lived in new ways in every age. The church must learn to express God's unchanging truth in ways that can be heard within our culture today and to bear witness to the faith in ways that are seen as authentic by people of our times.

The more we remove the obstacles in the way—our fears, our complacency, our cultural blocks, our false assumptions, and our lack of understanding—the more we will experience the transforming effects of the word of God. As we unlock the bolts and open the way to Christ, we will allow him to cross the threshold and we will experience a life that is worth living forever.

Crossing the Threshold When the Door Is Locked

Although we lock the door of our lives and block the way to Christ's entry, the risen Lord does not wait until we have removed all the obstacles for him to enter our lives. In the resurrection account of John's gospel, the evangelist writes:

> *Although the doors of the house where the disciples met were locked, Jesus came and stood among them and said, "Peace be with you."* [JOHN 20:19, 26]

The disciples had bolted the door out of fear, but that presented no barrier for the Risen One. Jesus came and stood among them, offering them forgiveness and peace. He speaks to them the word of life, and they are healed and renewed.

Jesus can come through our locked doors and present himself to us and speak to us. Any openness in our mind or heart is sufficient space for his entry. We will remain fearful, misunderstanding, and reluctant, but he continually offers his healing and peace. Although we sometimes feel that we need to have our life in order for Jesus to come in, he doesn't wait. He comes despite the locked doors.

Jesus didn't demand that Peter, Andrew, James, and John clear up all their selfishness and misunderstandings before he called them to discipleship. Jesus called the Samaritan woman despite her reluctance and her sins. Jesus didn't say to Zacchaeus, "Change your life and then God will love you." In actions more than words, Jesus showed Zacchaeus that God yearns to enter his heart and is drawing near with love. "I must stay at your house today," Jesus said to the chief tax collector, and the life of Zacchaeus was turned inside out by being in the presence of Jesus, because he realized that his sinfulness and greed were no barrier to divine love.

The foundation of God's word is the fact that God is able to be known and wants to be known by us. Because we are created by God and for God, God never ceases to draw us to himself. Only in God's self-revelation will we find the truth and happiness we never stop searching for. Only through Jesus can we experience the fullness of life for which we long. Because we are inclined by our nature toward transcendent truth and goodness, we can only prevent ourselves from experiencing God's life through the obstructions we put in the way. Yet, however much we cloud our perceptions and obscure the evidence of God's presence, God's word continues to seek entry.

The Life-changing Power of God's Word

The word of God, the divine communication to which all people are called to listen and that everyone is invited to receive, is the foundation of human life. Because we are created and sustained by God's word, it contains our truest purpose and our ultimate goal. Yet responding to God's word in faith is not just a personal choice among the many options that life offers us. The response of faith is our acceptance of what God intends for us.

The word of God is powerful because it is so much more than a word. It contains a mighty inner dynamic. It communicates God's healing strength, saving authority, and divine life. When we receive God's word into our lives with anticipation and expectation, we can expect to be changed.

The Scriptures express the transforming power of God's word in many ways. Jeremiah declares that the voice of God speaking to people and that inner voice speaking within us is an intense and penetrating fire, an announcement that shatters our conventional ideas and comfortable ways of thinking:

Is not my word like fire, says the Lord, and like a
hammer that breaks a rock into pieces? [JER 23:29]

The psalmist describes God's word as a luminous beacon that guides our way through life's darkness. Our pathway becomes illumined by God's guiding presence showing us the way.

> *Your word is a lamp to my feet and a light to my path.*
> {PSALM 119:105}

Jesus teaches that God's word is like seed planted in soil. When the rocks are removed and the choking thorns pulled up, it grows and bears fruit. When we cultivate the word in our hearts, it produces results within our lives.

> *The sower sows the word...And these are the ones sown*
> *on the good soil: they hear the word and accept it and*
> *bear fruit, thirty and sixty and a hundredfold.*
> {MARK 4:14, 20}

The letter to the Hebrews states that God's word penetrates into the deepest part of our being, like a piercing sword. Everything within us is laid bare, and nothing can remain hidden from God's penetrating power.

> *The word of God is living and active, sharper than*
> *any two-edged sword, piercing until it divides soul*
> *from spirit, joints from marrow; it is able to judge the*
> *thoughts and intentions of the heart.* {HEB 4:12}

When we prayerfully and receptively read the great living book of sacred Scripture, our lives cannot remain the same. The more we remove the obstacles, the more powerfully Scripture will change us. Sometimes these changes are overwhelming; more often they are subtle and gradual. Sometimes others notice the gradual transformation within us before we do. But the fruit of studying the Bible is always the fruit of the Spirit: "love, joy, peace, patience, kindness, generosity, faithfulness, gentleness, and self-control" (Galatians 5:22–23). When we begin to notice this fruit in the way we live our lives each day, we will know that the word of God is working within us.

Disciples as Bearers of the Word of God

Jesus' invitation to discipleship involves hearing his knock, listening to his voice, and letting him through the doorway of our lives. At the beginning of each gospel, Jesus calls disciples to come and follow him, to learn from him, and to share deeply in his life. But at the end of the gospels, Jesus offers another call, an invitation not to "come" but to "go"—go and witness, go and make disciples, go and proclaim the good news.

So the life of Christian discipleship moves in both directions. We must listen to God's word and witness to God's word. We welcome Jesus into our lives, then we go out to do the work of God's kingdom. We open the door of our lives to let Jesus in, then we go out across that threshold to be his disciples and witnesses in the world.

The book of Revelation offers us the image with which we began, the closed door with Jesus standing outside and knocking.

> *Listen! I am standing at the door, knocking; if you hear my voice and open the door, I will come into you and eat with you, and you with me.* [REV 3:20]

In this passage, Jesus is waiting at the door for us to open our lives to him. When we open the door and invite him across the threshold, he will nourish our lives with abundance.

The book of Revelation also offers us another image of Jesus at the doorway. Here Jesus himself opens the door with the key of his authority as Messiah and Lord.

These are the words of the holy one, the true one,
who has the key of David,
who opens and no one will shut,
who shuts and no one opens:
"I know your works. Look, I have set before you an open
door, which no one is able to shut." [REV 3:7–8]

As the one who has the divine authority to open and shut the door (Isa 22:22), the Risen One declares to his hearers, "I have set before you an open door." This is the doorway through which disciples will be witnesses to God's word. After disciples open the door to the Lord, he himself presents an open door for them through which the good news will be shared with the world.

Paul also uses the image of the open door as a metaphor for his missionary activity. He writes to the Corinthians, "A wide door for effective work has opened to me" (1 Cor 16:9), and "A door was opened for me in the Lord" (2 Cor 2:12). Paul also urges the Christians in Colossae to pray "that God will open to us a door for the word" (Col 4:3). This door for the proclamation of the good news of Christ is open to all disciples and stands as a divine invitation to witness to the word of God.

Understanding Scripture through the biblical imagery of the door and the threshold offers us a new perspective on the Christian experience of Bible study. Inviting Jesus, the Word of God, through the doorway is a personal and invitational way of approaching sacred Scripture. Responding to his knocking on the door and letting him cross the threshold into our lives is a magnificent way of imagining his call to listen to the word of God. And crossing the threshold to go out of our inner life and into the world is a wonderful way of envisioning his call to witness to the word of God.

In the following chapters we will look at ways of crossing

over several different kinds of thresholds as we open our lives to the study of Scripture. Our coming and going across the threshold will deepen our understanding of God's word and our ability to hear and witness to the good news it offers to us and to the world.

❖ ❖ ❖

KEYS FOR UNLOCKING THE DOOR

When we hear Jesus knocking, listen to his voice, and allow him to enter through the doorway of our lives, we become his disciples and live in his presence.

The good news offered by God's word is the invitation to a new and transformed life.

The Bible is not intended to be complex, controversial, or confining, but rather to be captivating.

The unchanging Christian faith must be thought out afresh and expressed in new ways in every age.

We don't have to unlock all the bolts ourselves. The risen Jesus comes to us despite locked doors.

God deeply wants to be known by us and never ceases to draw us to the divine presence, the beginning and goal of our lives.

After disciples listen to God's word, Jesus presents an open doorway for disciples to go forth and witness to God's word.

❖ ❖ ❖

QUESTIONS FOR REFLECTION AT THE THRESHOLD

- In what ways have I experienced a call like that of the fishermen, the Samaritan woman, or Zacchaeus?

- What must I leave behind in order to follow Jesus as his disciple?

- In what ways do I experience the word of God and the gospel message as good news?

- What are the bolts on the door of my life that require unlocking?

- What is my life's deepest longing? How do I experience God in the midst of my desires?

- Which Scripture passage best convinces me of the life-changing power of God's word?

- What does Jesus want me to do as he opens the door for me to witness and evangelize?

PRAYER FOR CROSSING THE THRESHOLD

Lord Jesus, you pass through my locked door and enter into my life. Draw me to yourself and give me a desire to be your disciple. Show me what I need to leave behind to follow you with all my heart. Enable me to listen to God's word and be transformed through its saving power. Then teach me to witness to that word and share the good news of your life with the world.

Crossing the Threshold...

3 From Paper and Ink to the Living Word of God

AS MOSES PASSED THROUGH THE WILDERNESS AND SAW THE BURNING BUSH BENEATH THE MOUNTAIN, HE WAS ON THE THRESHOLD OF AN ENCOUNTER WITH THE LIVING GOD. The fiery bush, burning but not consumed, was God's instrument to bring Moses from his ordinary life to an experience of God's living word.

> *God called to him out of the bush, "Moses, Moses!" and he said, "Here I am." Then he said, "Come no closer! Remove the sandals from your feet, for the place on which you are standing is holy ground."* {**EXOD 3:4–5**}

God wanted Moses to remove his shoes in order to prepare himself to be ready for this divine encounter. Planting his feet firmly in the earth and ready to listen, Moses began to hear God's revelation and opened his heart to the message.

27

In many cultures of the world today, people remove their shoes at the door of their homes. They leave their footwear at the threshold before entering the sacred domestic space. The same is true for the entryway to temples and places of prayer. Pilgrims remove their traveling boots and enter the holy sanctuary unshod in order to prepare themselves to experience the transcendent presence.

When we prepare to read the Bible, we are like Moses before the burning bush. The word of God is fiery but never consumed, effective but never depleted. We can prepare ourselves for this encounter with God by leaving our day-to-day concerns at the doorway and stepping into the experience with a sense of expectation burning in our hearts. And like Moses, when we listen to God speaking to us through Scripture, we can expect to be changed in some way by that encounter. God's living word always calls us to a deeper, richer, and fuller life.

This holy ground will become a place we want to visit often. The world of Scripture is our sacred place, the living expression of God speaking with us. When we read the Bible with open hearts, we bring ourselves into the text and become participants within the sacred space. We enter personally into the story of salvation that God is continually shaping.

The Shape of the Sacred Text
In the ancient world, biblical texts were written on long scrolls made of a thin, paperlike material from the papyrus plant. Although papyrus was relatively easy to produce, it was delicate and not very pliable. Often long scrolls were required for large-volume texts, but these scrolls were fragile and did not last many years.

In the Greco-Roman world it became common to cut sheets from papyrus rolls into pages. The original book, or codex, was formed by binding these sheets together, which was generally an improvement over the scroll. Papyrus was replaced by parchment, made from dried and treated animal skins. This was much more durable, especially in the more moist climates of Europe. The earliest complete Bibles still in existence are parchment codices from the fourth century. However, many papyrus and parchment manuscripts of individual books and thousands of fragments exist from much earlier times.

Of course, all of these ancient texts were written by hand, a very slow and meticulous process. It would require several hours for a good scribe to write one page. These handwritten biblical texts were costly and rare. They were found in the libraries of religious communities, and occasionally they were possessed by wealthy or influential individuals.

For the masses of Christian faithful through the ages, most of whom were illiterate and unable to read the biblical texts, church art and architecture have displayed the biblical story of salvation. Byzantine mosaics display the scenes of Scripture in a wondrous way, and Gothic cathedrals present the Bible in stone and glass. In the Middle Ages, monasteries produced both texts and biblical art as they created illuminated pages of Scripture. In the scriptoriums, monks meticulously copied the pages of the sacred text onto fine parchment, and they illuminated the pages with gold leaf, brilliant colors, and exquisite miniature art.

With the invention of the printing press in the fifteenth century, it became increasingly possible to mass-produce copies of the Bible. In fact, the Gutenberg Bible was the first book ever to be printed with moveable type in the West. Although these early printed Bibles were significantly cheaper than manuscript Bibles, most professors, students, and people of ordinary income would have been unable to afford them. But increasingly in recent centuries, Bibles have become inexpensive and are translated into almost every known language in the world.

Today we have mass-produced paperback Bibles, online electronic Bibles, and even Bible apps. This ready availability of Scripture can cause us to be rather casual about this great treasure. We do well to stop and consider the fact that we can hold in our hands this ancient instrument of God's revelation. The same inspired Scriptures are contained in these modern media as in the ancient, priceless manuscripts. From this ink and paper and from these digital texts springs the ageless word of life, the gospel of love.

A Personal and Relational Word

Although God's self-revelation comes to us through paper and ink and digital texts, the sacred texts are a personal reality. The Scriptures are far more than a collection of historical documents and literary masterpieces. Because God wants to be personally known to humanity, divine revelation is relational to the core. Every text of Scripture can be understood as God speaking with God's people, inviting them to a deeper and more personal relationship.

Because God's revelation is personal, we are called to be personally involved in this divine self-communication. Every word we read in Scripture involves us relationally. All the images, metaphors, stories, adventures, symbols, poems, songs, and prayers presented to us on the biblical pages pull us into participation and lead us to a personal involvement with God.

Reading the Bible, then, is a real encounter with God. God manifests the divine self to us through the long history of salvation, which is expressed in the inspired Scriptures. God speaks to us as a family, and invites us to share in divine life. Scripture is a privileged way in which we can come to know God more fully.

Every time we open the Bible, then, our hearts should tremble a bit, wondering what we will hear as God speaks to us through the sacred text. We can prepare ourselves for each encounter by repeating the words of Samuel as we turn the pages: "Speak, Lord, for your servant is listening" (1 Sam 3:9–10). Some of the saints and spiritual masters of old prayed and fasted before taking in hand the sacred and priceless manuscripts. Should we not at least invite God to open our ears and our hearts to truly listen to this word?

The Bible is indeed a treasury of literature, preserving the hallowed memories of our Israelite and Christian ancestors. But it is also a living word, a word filled with God's Spirit. And we believe that when we take this text in our hands, we encounter the word of God. We proclaim in liturgy, "The word of the Lord," "The Gospel of the Lord." When we listen for the voice of the Lord, we can truly encounter God's word and respond in faith.

The "God-breathed" Scriptures

The divinely revealed realities that are presented to us in the text of sacred Scripture have been written down under the inspiration of the Holy Spirit. Paul says, "All Scripture is inspired by God" (2 Tim 3:16). In the Greek text, the word is *theo-pneustos*, "God-breathed." God's presence and life have been breathed into sacred Scripture. The breath of divine life has been placed in these words. Be assured that Paul's word is *theo-pneustos*, "God-breathed," and not *theo-graptos*, "God-written." God did not write the words of the texts, nor did God dictate the words to human beings. Rather, as in the ancient prophets, "men and women moved by the Holy Spirit spoke from God" (2 Pet 1:21).

While God did indeed work within the human authors of Scripture, inspiration is not just what God did in the minds and hearts of those biblical writers thousands of years ago. "God-breathed" also describes the Bible today. The sacred texts are always inspired; they are always filled with the Spirit of God. Because Scripture is inspired, the voice of God is heard, sounding through the biblical pages and into our hearts. Because of the indwelling Spirit, the word is alive and charged with divine power to change and renew us.

A deep spiritual union is formed between the human author of the text, who was moved by the Spirit to write, and the prayerful reader of the inspired page, who is moved by that same Holy Spirit when reading it. The difference in time does not matter, because both are joined to the living word animated by the same Holy Spirit. Of course, the work of the human authors is finished, but because their words are penetrated by the life-giving Spirit, their writing is forever living.

Through inspiration, Scripture is always youthful, offering us new insights, challenges, and renewal. The Holy Spirit continues to breathe life and power into the sacred texts, so that on every page we can truly encounter the living word of God. As God made his presence known and spoke to Moses through the burning bush, God meets us on the holy ground of these inspired pages and shares divine life with us.

The Word of God in the Words of Human Authors

In these biblical texts, God is speaking, so much so that we can say that God is the truest author of Scripture. Yet, at the same time, God chose certain human writers, inspiring them to write and to express God's own self-revelation to humanity.

Because God inspired human authors, who wrote with their own faculties, vocabulary, and style, we experience God's self-communication in a very human way, in a way we can understand. In the inspired Scriptures, God communicates with us in a sacramental way, through the earthly material of human life. The Scriptures share in the incarnational reality of the Christian faith, in which the human and divine embrace. In the sacred texts, God communicates divine life and truth to humanity, but we experience it gradually in human history, through human authors, with human words and deeds.

Because we trust in God's inspiration of Scripture, we believe that the Bible is truly the word of God in human words. While God communicates authoritatively through the Bible, the language of the biblical texts is not capable of containing or capturing the fullness of God.

This sacramental understanding of biblical inspiration prevents us from falling into the distortions of fundamentalism. A fundamentalist interpretation of Scripture does not sufficiently take into account the incarnational reality of the Bible, the human authorship and the historical origins and development of the Scriptures. A fundamentalist reading lifts texts out of their context, placing undue stress on what they seem to say on the surface, often insisting that every word of Scripture is historically and scientifically exact, holding the ancient texts to our modern definitions of accuracy.

What God teaches in Scripture is divine truth—a reality that is far wider and deeper than our modern categories of fact and information. So texts must always be interpreted contextually—within their historical and cultural context, as well as within the context of the other parts of Scripture and the church's ongoing tradition. The books of the Bible faithfully teach the truth that God reveals in Scripture for our salvation.

By understanding God's inspiration of Scripture, we can trust in the truth of biblical texts without trying to turn them into something they are not. Faithful study of the texts seeks to go beneath their surface to determine the essential and timeless truth of the message. St. Jerome wrote that the Bible must be read and interpreted "in the light of the same Spirit by whom it was written."[1] Because the Bible is inspired, it is trustworthy. It might not reveal the fullness of its truth automatically to every casual reader, but with time, the guidance of the church, and good Bible studies, we can trust the Bible to offer us the truth that God wants to reveal to us.

Provocative Questions for Opening Doors

Communication with others and with God is essential for helping us locate the keys for entering the door of our inner temple. Among the means that God uses for opening the door are questions that are stimulating and challenging.

After Moses removes his sandals at the sight of the burning bush, God begins the self-revelation by generating two questions within Moses that lead to further revelation. The first question of Moses is "Who am I that I should go to Pharaoh and bring the Israelites out of Egypt?" And the second question is "If I come to the Israelites and tell them, 'The God of your ancestors has sent me to you,' and they ask me, 'What is his name?' what shall I say to them?"

In responding to each of the questions of Moses, God does not give a direct or definitive answer. Instead of giving a response that is neatly wrapped in a box, God responds in a way that elicits more questions, or that tells Moses that his questions will be answered through his experience with God, or that gives Moses more confidence in his abilities to answer the questions himself.

In response to Moses' question "Who am I?" God replies, "I will be with you." In other words, God tells Moses that he will discover why he was chosen through the experiences that will unfold. In response to Moses' question about who God is, God replies, "I AM WHO I AM." Obviously this is not a name by which God could be defined. Rather, this enigmatic name affirms that God is unfathomable and beyond understanding. God can only be known by revealing the divine nature through God's action in the unfolding of history. In response to these questions, Moses is invited to cross the threshold into a lifelong and committed relationship with God.

The dialogue established by provocative questions draws us beyond our status-quo lives and leads us into untraveled terrain. Through these kinds of questions, we are awakened to new ways we are called to change. These kinds of penetrating questions help us to face the unknown and are essential for opening the door to a deeper life with God.

Throughout the four gospels, Jesus is asked numerous questions. But how many questions does Jesus directly answer? Usually Jesus does one of three things when asked a question. He either remains silent, as when he is questioned by Pilate at his trial; or he responds with another question, as when asked whether to pay taxes to Caesar and Jesus replies by asking whose head is on the coin; or he tells a story, as when the lawyer asks Jesus "And who is my neighbor?" and Jesus replies with the parable of the good samaritan.

Jesus' idea of making disciples is not about giving people answers. Rather, it is about leading them to the threshold, where they will yearn for wisdom and seek a deeper longing for God. Good questions should propel us inward. If we wish to grow in relationship to God, we must be willing to ask penetrating questions of ourselves and to grapple with them. Easy answers put us in control, whereas provocative questions allow God to lead and encourage us on to spiritual maturity.

The study of the Bible elicits many questions that have no easy answers. Through the divine word, God wants to break his people out of their dualistic minds—their black-and-white, either-or thinking. The response of Jesus was usually both-and, not either-or. Many of the religious leaders of his day thought that the purpose of faith was to give people answers. But, as a true teacher, Jesus was not an answer man. He tried to move people away from believing that God wants us to know all the answers so we can achieve doctrinal certainty, and toward the view that penetrating questions unlock the door to deeper self-knowledge and communion with God.

A successful Bible study thrives on good, provocative questions for reflection. Several types of questions appeal to different layers of the human person addressed by God's word. First, questions help the reader ruminate on the text. They ask us to go back and focus on some aspect of what we've read so that it enters our memory. Second, questions ask the reader to probe more deeply. They challenge us to create a dialogue between the text and what we know from other life experiences. Third, questions challenge readers to apply their learning in practical ways. These three types of questions appeal to the intellectual, affective, and behavioral aspects of our personalities. Very simply, they move our head, our heart, and our hands, orienting us to a fuller life and relationship with God.

The dialogue elicited by stimulating questions helps us experience Scripture as the living word of God. There is no final word when it comes to studying Scripture, because the last word is a dead word. The living word of God continually confronts us with new realizations and new challenges. As Moses wrestled with unanswered questions, he grew in his understanding of both himself and God. With unshod feet he crossed the threshold into the deep mystery of God and became a great instrument of God's saving word for the world.

❖ ❖ ❖

KEYS FOR UNLOCKING THE DOOR

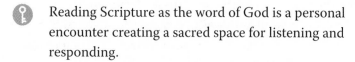 Reading Scripture as the word of God is a personal encounter creating a sacred space for listening and responding.

The movement from papyrus scrolls, to parchment codex, to printed book, to digital text challenges us to consider our relationship to the changeless word of God.

Every text of Scripture expresses God's speaking with humanity, inviting and compelling people into a deeper and more personal relationship.

The Holy Spirit continues to breathe life and power into the sacred texts, so that we can truly encounter the living, renewing word of God.

As the word of God in the words of human authors, Scripture participates in the incarnational and sacramental reality of the Christian faith in which the human and divine embrace.

Penetrating questions without easy answers unlock the door to deeper self-knowledge and spiritual maturity.

The questions we ask of Scripture convince us that the text is a living word, continually confronting us with new realizations and new challenges.

❖ ❖ ❖

QUESTIONS FOR REFLECTION AT THE THRESHOLD

- In what ways can the encounter of Moses with God at the burning bush teach me how to experience Scripture as the word of God?

- In what way does the medium (i.e., gold-leafed pages, paperback, or app) for reading Scripture affect my understanding of and appreciation for the word of God?

- How can I make my reading of Scripture a more personal encounter with God?

- In what sense does the truth that Scripture is "God-breathed" animate my reading under the guidance of the Holy Spirit?

- How does an understanding of the human authorship, personal style, individual vocabulary, and historical context prevent a fundamentalist reading of Scripture?

- What is the question I most often ask myself? Is this question effective for leading me to a deeper life with God?

- What is it like for me to sit with a question and not have a definitive answer?

PRAYER FOR CROSSING THE THRESHOLD

Spirit of the Living God, you have breathed into the sacred pages of Scripture, and you guide my life as a disciple of Jesus. Teach me through questions and reflection how to grow in faith, to deepen my trust, and to continually renew the divine life within me. May I always experience God's word as enlivening, youthful, relational, and transforming.

Crossing the Threshold...

4 From Bondage and Death to Freedom and Life

THE HEART OF THE BIBLE IS THE CROSSING OF THE THRESH-OLD FROM BONDAGE AND DEATH TO FREEDOM AND LIFE. This basic pattern of the threshold experience is played out over and over again throughout salvation history. People find themselves imprisoned, locked in captivity; and God, with power and compassion, opens the door so that they will experience deliverance and abundant life.

This bondage takes many forms and many names in Scripture: slavery, imprisonment, oppression, grief, doubt, sin, death, alienation, and despair. Likewise, the passage across the threshold takes many forms and names: rescue, deliverance, ransom, release, passover, redemption, and salvation. This deliverance that God offers may be physical or spiritual, temporal or eternal.

In the Old Testament, God's people are continually rescued

from peril and harm as an expression of God's covenant relationship with them. In the New Testament, this divine ransom is extended to all people. God desires everyone to experience the divine offer of freedom and life. Through the prayerful reading of Scripture, every person comes to the threshold, ready to personally accept this salvation, crossing over through Jesus Christ and his church.

The Exodus, Israel's Passageway to Freedom and Life

One of the most important descriptions of God in the Hebrew Scriptures is "I am the Lord your God, who brought you out of the land of Egypt, out of the house of slavery" (Exod 20:2; Deut 5:6). The liberation of God's people from bondage and their establishment as a people was the decisive event of God's self-revelation to Israel. God's momentous act of salvation forms the heart of the Old Testament and the pattern for all future experiences of divine deliverance.

God initiates the events of the exodus as God sees the wretched state of the people and hears them as they cry out for God's help. After revealing the divine name to Moses at the burning bush, God says,

> I have observed the misery of my people who are
> in Egypt; I have heard their cry on account of their
> taskmasters. Indeed, I know their sufferings, and I
> have come down to deliver them from the Egyptians,
> and to bring them up out of that land to a good and
> broad land, a land flowing with milk and honey.
> [EXOD 3:7–8]

The passage that Israel will experience in the exodus is not just a rescue from oppression; it also includes the freedom to live in a land of blessing and abundance. The fertile and spacious land of God's promise is the ultimate goal of Israel's deliverance.

The passage of God's people from Egypt to the promised land is narrated in a series of threshold events. First, God's enslaved people are rescued from their oppression on the night of Passover. As the tenth and final plague comes upon the Egyptians, families of the Israelites are instructed to sacrifice a lamb and to apply its blood to the lintel and the doorposts of their homes. This sacrificial blood at the threshold prevents death from entering their houses and becomes the doorway through which the families of God would enter their freedom.

Then, after God's people have escaped from Egyptian bondage, they come to the sea, with the Egyptian army in hot pursuit. At God's command, Moses stretches out his hand over the sea, and the waters are divided, allowing the Israelites to pass through the sea for their final escape to freedom. With the waters divided like a wall to their right and left, the Israelites passed through on dry land just before the break of dawn.

This passage of Israel through the sea is remembered as the primary event of salvation for Israel, symbolically expressing the whole narrative of transition from bondage to freedom. For the ancient Israelites, the sea represented the forces of destruction, chaos, and death. The passage through the waters, from the darkness into the dawn, is an image of birthing, the transition through the birth canal. Israel is God's firstborn son, and the exodus is described by later writers as the moment of their birth.

The song of Moses in Exodus 15 celebrates God's magnificent rescue at the sea and describes this liberation as the way God will be continually manifested. God is the one who is repeatedly conquering all those forces opposed to freedom and abundant life: crushing injustice, overcoming domination, and vanquishing oppression. The newborn Israelites praise their God of freedom and life and celebrate God's divine victory over all the forces of oppression and death. The song links

Israel's "coming out" of bondage to the people's "coming into" the promised land.

The final threshold moment of the exodus occurs after the forty-year sojourn in the wilderness and after the death of Moses. God leads the people under the direction of Joshua from the wilderness, across the Jordan River, and into the promised land. This grand procession of Israel into Canaan is the crossing over the threshold, the entranceway into "a good and broad land, a land flowing with milk and honey." God's people can now trust and worship their Savior, who has led them into freedom and abundant life.

God's Deliverance throughout Israel's History

The people of Israel learned to reflect on all the events of their national history in light of the primary event of the exodus. This passage from bondage and death to freedom and life became the paradigm for describing all of God's future actions. The Israelites expressed their faith in God by reciting the saving deeds they experienced throughout their history, beginning with the exodus and narrating their history with ever-new hope. Because God had heard the people's cries in the past, they could be certain that God would continue to rescue and save them. In every age, Israel knew that its future would take shape according to the same patterns with which its past had been formed.

For example, at the time when the exodus narratives were being written in their final form, the Israelites were experiencing a new captivity and a new exodus. From the bondage of their exile in Babylon, God led them out of their captivity and again brought them through the wilderness back to their homeland. This return from exile is described in the prophets and other historical books with the same vocabulary of bondage and divine redemption that we read in the Torah. Through the prophet Jeremiah comes the word of the Lord: "Do not be dismayed, O Israel; for I am going to save you from far away, and your offspring from the land of their captivity" (Jer 30:10). The exodus experience was never just a memory of the past for God's people; it was a living reality for every generation. When the people of Israel reenacted the Passover each year, through the sacrifice of a lamb in the temple and the seder meal in their homes, it made the redeeming event present again. Through the timeless rituals of the liturgy, the saving power of the past event became real and personal for each new generation. They applied the blood of the lamb on the lintel and doorposts of their home, and they gathered with their family to retell the story while eating the Passover meal. It was as though all the past and future generations of Israel came together on this evening of Passover to be reconstituted as the redeemed people of God.

Because God freed his people, the whole society of ancient Israel was commanded by God to embody this divine redeeming compassion in their relationships with one another. They were to treat the aliens and immigrants in the land with kindness because the Israelites were once aliens in a foreign land. This divine compassion was to be extended by the Israelites to all the widows and orphans, the weak and the suffering, because God has compassion on those who are defenseless and vulnerable.

The go'el or "redeemer" was a close male relative who had the responsibility of rescuing (redeeming) his blood-relatives from situations of crisis or difficulty. He would buy back their mortgaged property or buy them out of slavery. These purchases would free the person and restore the unity of the family. This divine mandate of redemption implements in society the work of God as the divine redeemer of his people.

Every time the people of Israel found themselves in an experience of bondage or trouble, they looked to God for an experience of liberation in a new and ever more powerful way. The psalms declare that God is Israel's liberator from their enemies (69:18), their redeemer from oppression and violence (72:14), their rescuer from the pit of death (103:4), and the one who will ransom Israel "from all its iniquities" (130:8).

The prophet Isaiah calls God by the titles "Savior" and "Redeemer" (Isa 60:16). God speaks of this saving power as never-ending: "My deliverance will be forever and my salvation to all generations" (Isa 51:8). And Job, in the midst of all his suffering and abandonment, declares with a mighty trust, "I know that my Redeemer lives" (Job 19:25).

God's Anointed One and Servant Manifests God's Redemption

After the exile, God's people began to look toward a future Anointed One (Messiah) to finally deliver them from bondage and establish the time of salvation. Isaiah speaks of him as one from the royal lineage of David, the one named Immanuel (Isa 7:14). He is a light that will shine upon a people in darkness, the one who will break the yoke of oppression from the shoulders of God's people, and the Prince of Peace (Isa 9:2–6). He will grow from the root of Jesse, the Spirit of the Lord will rest upon him, and he will judge the poor with righteousness (Isa 11:1–4). The mission of God's Anointed is proclaimed by the prophet:

> *The spirit of the Lord God is upon me,*
> *because the Lord has anointed me;*
> *he has sent me to bring good news to the oppressed,*
> *to bind up the broken-hearted,*
> *to proclaim liberty to the captives,*
> *and release to the prisoners.* {ISA 61:1}

Other prophetic passages speak of a Servant of the Lord who

inaugurates God's reign. This Servant not only restores the people of Israel, but is "a light to the nations" so that God's salvation reaches "to the end of the earth" (Isa 49:6). Yet he is a suffering Servant, experiencing shame and disgrace. He suffers not only for his mission, but for the sake of the very ones inflicting suffering upon him. Endowed with the spirit of God, he suffers both in the place of others and for their deliverance. Without violence, deceit, or vengeance, "like a lamb that is led to the slaughter," he pours out himself to death, and bears the sins of many (Isa 53:5–12).

The figures of God's Anointed One and the Servant of the Lord developed separately in the prophetic literature, yet they began to merge closer to the time of Jesus. And during the New Testament period they converge in Jesus, whose identity is seen to fulfill the expectations in both of these figures. The time of salvation, not only for Israel but for the whole world, comes in Jesus.

As the Scriptures demonstrate, God's mission is the salvation of the world from corruption, sin, death, guilt, meaninglessness, and despair. God's people looked toward a future that would fulfill their every hope. This mission of God comes to its completion in Jesus the Messiah, the suffering Servant of God.

Jesus Provides the Threshold for All

The gospels show us that Jesus proclaimed in word and deed that the kingdom of God is at hand. This reign of God in the world is marked by freedom and life: "the blind receive their sight, the lame walk, the lepers are cleansed, the deaf hear, the dead are raised, and the poor have the good news brought to them" (Matt 11:5). When Jesus entered the synagogue at Nazareth, he read from the scroll of Isaiah: "The Spirit of the Lord is upon me, because he has anointed me to bring good news to the poor. He has sent me to proclaim release to captives and recovery of sight to the blind, to let the oppressed go free" (Luke 4:18). Then he proclaimed, "Today this Scripture has been fulfilled in your hearing." Jesus, the Anointed One, is bringing the hopes of God's people to completion and providing the threshold for all to enter into the fullness of freedom and life.

The liberating mission of Jesus' life comes to its summit at his passion, when Jesus shows himself to be the suffering Servant of God who came "to give his life as a ransom for many" (Mark 10:45). Because Jesus suffers in the place of others, offering his life in sacrifice for the world, God redeems humanity from the forces of evil and the power of sin. The death and resurrection of Jesus is our pathway from an existence doomed to death into a life that is full and eternal. The stone rolled across the doorway of Jesus' tomb marks the threshold between bondage and liberation, between death and life.

Paul describes this saving work accomplished by Jesus as a movement from slavery to freedom, and he urges the people of his communities to safeguard the liberty that the Lord has earned for them: "For freedom Christ has set us free. Stand firm, therefore, and do not submit again to a yoke of slavery" (Gal 5:1). He describes our redemption as a passing over from darkness into the kingdom, from the captivity of sin to freedom experienced through forgiveness:

> *[The Father] has rescued us from the power of darkness*
> *and transferred us into the kingdom of his beloved Son,*
> *in whom we have redemption, the forgiveness of sins.*
> {Col 1:13–14}

God's Liberating Energy at the Threshold

The Acts of the Apostles narrates two accounts in which the leading apostles, Peter and Paul, are liberated by God from prison. The story of Peter shows him captive in maximum security, with one soldier chained to each of his arms and two others guarding the door, while the church prays for him. But God acts through the ministry of an angel to rescue him during the feast of Passover. God frees him from the darkness with a shining light, saves him from imminent death, and brings him forth to continue his ministry in Jerusalem (Acts 12:1–11).

Peter's emergence from prison has clear parallels to God's liberation of the Israelites at Passover and Jesus' emergence from the tomb. Peter's crossing the threshold from imprisonment to new life, with the iron gate of the prison opening through divine power, demonstrates that God's action in Jesus, his death and resurrection, continues to empower his disciples.

Paul, along with his companion Silas, is imprisoned in Philippi, and the other prisoners and guards listen to them praying and singing hymns. The fetters of all the prisoners are unfastened and the doors are opened through a powerful earthquake. The jailer realizes the divine power at work, falls down trembling, and asks Paul, "What must I do to be saved?" (Acts 16:25–34).

This account demonstrates not only God's liberation of Paul and Silas, but more importantly, the divine deliverance of the jailer and his household. While the jailer brought them to his home and washed their wounds, Paul and Silas spoke "the word of the Lord" to him and all in his house, inviting them, "Believe on the Lord Jesus, and you will be saved, you and your household." The entire family was baptized; they all shared a meal together and all were filled with the joy of salvation. Again, the redeeming power of Jesus' death and resurrection, the transforming power of the gospel, and God's liberating grace are at work in the ministry of the church.

The essence of Scripture, the heart of the good news for humanity, is the announcement that God has provided the doorway to salvation for all people. We cross the threshold by hearing the word of God and responding to God's invitation to be transformed by divine grace. It is this divine grace that opens the "door of faith" (Acts 14:27) for us, ushering us into the life of communion with God and offering entry into the church.

While Jesus Christ provides the threshold for all people, his invitation to enter into the freedom and joy of salvation requires a human response. Salvation is God's ongoing work within us, but we must cooperate with divine grace through repentance, faith, and baptism. Repentance is our turning away from all the attitudes and actions that stand in the way of God and turning in the direction of God to experience the divine invitation to life. Faith is our response to God's offer, our acceptance of deliverance, entrusting our lives to Jesus Christ and following where he leads us. And baptism unites our lives to his death and resurrection. As Paul explains, "We have been buried with him by baptism into death, so that, just as Christ was raised from the dead by the glory of the Father, so we too might walk in newness of life" (Rom 6:4). In the waters of rebirth, our lives are incorporated into the life of Christ, making us children of the Father, destined to share in life forever.

Through repentance, faith, and baptism, in response to the grace of salvation offered to all people, we enter into the kingdom of God and into Christ's church. Following in the way of the One who came "to seek out and to save the lost" (Luke 19:10), we take on a responsibility to care for the defenseless, the poor, and the disenfranchised. The way of Jesus, who gave his whole life to redeem and save sinners, becomes the paradigm for the lives of his followers. With other Christians, we seek to love others as Christ has first loved us. As John tells members of his community, "We know love by this, that he laid down his life for us—and we ought to lay down our lives for one another" (1 John 3:16).

Entering through that door sets us on a journey that lasts

a lifetime. Salvation is not a single act, but an ongoing process. Paul encouraged his Philippian community to continue responding to the gift of salvation, recalling that divine grace is enabling them to live for God: "Work out your own salvation with fear and trembling; for it is God who is at work in you, enabling you both to will and to work for his good pleasure" (Phil 2:12–13). He assured the believers in Rome to continue along the Christian way of life with confident hope, "for salvation is nearer to us now than when we became believers" (Rom 13:11). Each day God calls us to believe a little more fervently, to search a little deeper, to become a little freer, always keeping in mind the joyful hope that Paul expressed from his prison cell:

I thank my God every time I remember you, constantly praying with joy in every one of my prayers for all of you, because of your sharing in the gospel from the first day until now. I am confident of this, that the one who began a good work among you will bring it to completion by the day of Jesus Christ. It is right for me to think this way about all of you, because you hold me in your heart, for all of you share in God's grace with me, both in my imprisonment and in the defense and confirmation of the gospel. For God is my witness, how I long for all of you with the compassion of Christ Jesus. And this is my prayer, that your love may overflow more and more with knowledge and full insight to help you to determine what is best, so that in the day of Christ you may be pure and blameless, having produced the harvest of righteousness that comes through Jesus Christ for the glory and praise of God.

{PHIL 1:3–11}

❖ ❖ ❖

KEYS FOR UNLOCKING THE DOOR

Through the prayerful reading of Scripture, we are invited to cross over from bondage by personally accepting the salvation God offers.

The liberation of God's people from bondage and the gift of freedom and blessings was the decisive event of salvation for Israel and the pattern for all future experiences of divine deliverance.

The Passover in Egypt, the passage through the sea, and the crossing over into the promised land express the threshold moments of the exodus experience.

The annual liturgy of Passover makes the saving event and its redemptive power present in every generation.

God's saving mission for the world is expressed in the prophets through the figures of God's Messiah and Servant.

The saving deeds of Jesus manifested the reign of God in the world by bringing people into an experience of freedom and life.

The liberating mission of Jesus comes to its peak at his passion and is completed in his resurrection.

❖ ❖ ❖

QUESTIONS FOR REFLECTION AT THE THRESHOLD

- What forms of bondage most inhibit me from experiencing life more fully?

- How does the experience of God's people in the exodus give hope to God's people in every age?

- In what ways is the moral code of God's people rooted in their experience of God's redeeming compassion?

- In what ways is the liberating energy of Christ's resurrection manifested in the ministry of Peter and Paul?

- How do I experience the redeeming and transforming power of Jesus' death and resurrection in the ministry of his church?

- Why does Christ's offer of salvation require from us the response of repentance, faith, and baptism?

- How does Paul teach that crossing the threshold to salvation is an ongoing, lifetime process?

❖ ❖ ❖

PRAYER FOR CROSSING THE THRESHOLD

God of Freedom and Life, you rescue your people from slavery, redeem us from sin, and save us from death. As you offer to me the doorway of salvation, help me respond to your grace by believing, searching, and hoping a little more each day. Lead me through the power of your dying and rising to the fullness of life.

Crossing the Threshold...

5 From Creation to New Creation

THE SWEEP OF SCRIPTURE, FROM GENESIS TO REVELATION, EXPRESSES GOD'S DESIRE TO OFFER THE FULLNESS OF LIFE TO THE WORLD. The opening two chapters of the Bible narrate that God, "in the beginning," created "the heavens and the earth" (Gen 1—2). And the final two chapters relate that God is establishing "a new heaven and a new earth" (Rev 21—22). These chapters frame the entire biblical narrative of the world's salvation. The process that God started is fulfilled as all creation is perfected and glorified according to God's plan.

Throughout the Bible's grand narrative, God is always making things new, leading people into richer and deeper experiences of salvation. God leads them from the covenant, relating to them with love and with mutual obligations, to the new covenant. God guides them from an experience of the temple in Jerusalem, promising to dwell with them there, to the new temple and the new Jerusalem. And God directs them from a creation marred by evil, sin, and death, to a new creation and, indeed, a new heaven and a new earth.

In the Bible's final book, God presents before the visionary an open door—"There in heaven a door stood open" (Rev 4:1)—and God invites him to cross the threshold and experience the divine presence. Before the throne of God, the visionary is shown the fulfillment of God's plan in Christ through a variety of biblical images and liturgical symbols. And finally, the one who sits on the throne says, "Behold, I am making all things new." Urging the visionary to record what he sees and hears, God says, "Write, for these words are faithful and true...It is done. I am the Alpha and the Omega, the beginning and the end" (Rev 21:5–6).

This framework of the whole Bible offers a context in which each book of the Bible can be interpreted. There is not a book within the whole collection of sacred books that can be interpreted satisfactorily in isolation from the rest. The Bible forms a grand narrative, and the central themes that run throughout the whole of Scripture offer us the big picture through which we can appreciate the details more clearly.

God's Desire to Dwell with People on Earth

The opening chapters of Genesis present us with God's intended design for the earth. The seven-day liturgical framework for God's creation, the formation of man and woman in the divine image, God's walking with them in the garden, and the forbidden tree of knowledge are all figurative expressions of what God most deeply desires for creation. God makes the garden the place of divine dwelling with man and woman, and as they continue to multiply and fill the earth, God wishes the whole world to be that divine dwelling place.

The Garden of Eden is described as a divine sanctuary where God is at home and lives in harmony with creation. Like ancient temples, it is entered through its east end where it is guarded by cherubim. God's command that the human being (the 'adam, in Hebrew) serve and care for the garden are the same verbs used in later passages to describe the duties of Israel's priests in the tabernacle. Human beings were designed by God to serve as priests in this garden-sanctuary, with direct access to God.

Similarly, God appoints the man and woman to be royal representatives, governing the earth on God's behalf. Their creation in the image of God confers regal status upon them. In the ancient world, the phrase "image of God" was linked to kings. The royal ruler was the living image of God in the world. This regal status is confirmed as God gives the man and woman dominion over every living thing, appointing them to rule with divine care and justice over God's creation. Just as a royal ruler set up his image in distant parts of his kingdom to indicate the extent of his authority, human beings are to perform a similar function in God's plan. As they are fruitful and their descendants spread throughout the earth, man and woman are to extend the reign of God throughout creation. God's original design for human beings is to make them a kingdom of priests and royal rulers throughout the earth.

The third chapter of Genesis shows that God's design is disrupted by the refusal of man and woman to live according to God's desire for creation. The cunning serpent represents the deceptive powers of evil within creation. The choice of man and woman to listen to the serpent's instructions rather than those of God is especially tragic in light of their royal and priestly status.

By failing to exercise their dominion over the serpent, they destroy the trusting harmony God desired within the garden-temple. In betraying God, man and woman are sent forth from the garden-temple, and they unleash the powers of evil to reign on the earth. Their God-given dominion over the creatures of the earth turns to destructive domination. God's authority is overturned, and harmony gives way to chaos. As the stories of Genesis continue to reveal, the hallmark of sinful humanity becomes violence toward other creatures, both human and animal, and toward the good creation.

Against this background (Gen 1—11), the whole history of salvation that follows in the biblical books expresses God's saving plan for how the world can become a dwelling place shared by God, humanity, and the creatures of the earth. God's people must be rescued from the control of evil and receive the royal and priestly dignity that God desires to bestow upon them. The kingdom of God must be established throughout the earth so that God may live with this royal and priestly people throughout the divine dwelling place on earth.

The Temple of God's Dwelling

As Genesis continues, God begins to redeem sinful humanity by calling Abraham and offering to him and his descendants a covenant relationship. With Abraham's obedience, God promises him countless offspring, a land for them to live in, and, most importantly, blessings to all the people of the earth through him. The remainder of Genesis shows God's relationship with Abraham's family in which God makes the divine presence known to them and reaffirms the covenant at sanctuaries throughout the land. For example, when Abraham shows his willingness to offer his son in sacrifice, God instructs him to build an altar on the sacred site of Mount Moriah. Later, when Jacob is traveling, he dreams of a ladder connecting heaven and earth, and God appears before him. Jacob builds an altar there and calls the place Bethel, which means "House of God."

In the book of Exodus, God enters into a covenant with the people at Mount Sinai and instructs them to build a tabernacle in the wilderness for God to dwell with them. The second half of the book consists of detailed directions for the construction of this lavish sanctuary. It consists of three distinct areas: a courtyard, a Holy Place entered from the east, and the Holy of Holies. Within the tabernacle, the Israelites constructed several sacred objects honoring the presence of God. In the Holy Place, they placed the menorah, the table of showbread, and the incense altar. In the Holy of Holies, separated by curtains embroidered with cherubim, they placed the ark of the covenant, called the footstool of God's heavenly throne. The tabernacle was made to be portable, so that it could be carried and reconstructed at every stop along the journey of God's people. Priests were appointed to serve and care for this sanctuary in the wilderness, which linked heaven and earth.

The end of Exodus states that at the completion of its construction, "the glory of the Lord filled the tabernacle." The divine presence, manifested as a cloud by day and fire by night, covered the dwelling while God's people encamped around it. Moses met with God here, though they were separated by the curtains. While the Israelites did not believe that God's being was restricted to the tabernacle or that God's presence was contained within it, they knew that the immanence of God was made perceptible and tangible there so that people could orient their minds and hearts to God.

When Israel entered the promised land, the tabernacle was set up at Shiloh. Yet, due to the sins of Israel and the corruption of its priests, God's presence departed from the sanctuary. The ark of the covenant was captured by Israel's enemies, but at God's direction, it was eventually returned and brought to Jerusalem. When David became king and captured Jerusalem, the ark was set up at the city's high place. Now the throne of the Israelite king and the footstool of the divine king were located next to each other in the same city.

However, David did not think it appropriate that his own royal residence should be grander than God's place of dwelling.

But God prohibited David from building a temple, promising that God would build a house for David (i.e., a dynasty) and that David's son would build a house for God (i.e., a temple). In time, David's son Solomon succeeded him to the throne and built a splendid temple in Jerusalem. Following Solomon's prayer dedicating the temple, God's glory filled the new sanctuary, the dwelling place of the Lord on earth.

Jerusalem is now the city of God. God's holiness extends from the temple to encompass the city. Those who dwell in Zion (a poetic name for Jerusalem) are blessed because of the Lord's presence there. Pilgrimage to Jerusalem provided an opportunity for them to come close to God and to celebrate God's relationship with them. Since God's ultimate desire is for the divine presence to fill the whole earth, Jerusalem is the beginning of this fulfillment. The city reflects in microcosm what God intends for the world.

Hope for a New Temple, a New Jerusalem, and a New Creation

The Old Testament story reaches its climax with the dedication of the temple during the reign of Solomon. Thereafter, we see a narrative of sustained decline, interrupted occasionally by the reigns of a few righteous kings in the dynasty of David. Eventually, the failure of God's people, along with their kings and priests, to live uprightly in the presence of God leads to the destruction of the temple and the conquest of Jerusalem by its enemies. During these centuries of decline, however, Israel's prophets keep hope alive and lead God's people to cross over to the experience of a new temple, a new Jerusalem, and even a new creation.

Isaiah received his prophetic calling during a vision of God in the Holy of Holies of the temple. The seraphim cried out, "Holy, holy, holy is the Lord of hosts; the whole earth is full of his glory," expressing the universal extent of God's holiness. The prophet's writings open with a description of the absolute corruption seizing Jerusalem before its destruction (Isa 1), but move quickly to a hopeful vision of the future when Zion will be established as the highest mountain "and all nations shall flow to it" in pilgrimage (Isa 2:2). Writing after the exile and the temple's destruction, Isaiah's disciple expressed hopes for a totally renewed Jerusalem:

> For I am about to create new heavens
>   and a new earth;
> the former things shall not be remembered
>   or come to mind.
> But be glad and rejoice forever
>   in what I am creating;
> for I am about to create Jerusalem as a joy,
>   and its people as a delight. [ISA 65:17–18]

The hope that God would complete this desire for creation lived on despite the destruction and loss experienced by God's people. In these prophetic verses, the creation of new heavens and a new earth is parallel to the creation of Jerusalem anew. This new creation has none of the deficiencies of the present one. Weeping and distress are no longer heard in the streets, the earth is fertile with abundant vineyards and food for all, the animals coexist in harmony, and God's presence provides everlasting light to the city.

The prophet Ezekiel received his calling while deported in exile. He envisions the throne of God coming toward him on a chariot, with God seated upon it in divine glory. The vision offers the prophet great hope that God has not abandoned the people. In the visions that follow, the prophet is shown how the glory of God departed the sanctuary in Jerusalem because of the idolatry, violence, and injustice committed there by the people (Ezek 8—10). Yet hope remains, and Ezekiel concludes with visions focusing on God's return to a restored land, a renewed Jerusalem, and a new temple. Ezekiel ends his idealized descriptions of this new city by giving it a new name: "And the name of the city from that time on shall be, The Lord is There" (Ezek 48:35). By expressing God's renewing power, the prophet communicates the hope that God remains committed to making the whole earth a divine dwelling.

Zechariah's prophetic words anticipate a transformed Jerusalem in which God will dwell: "Thus says the Lord: I will return to Zion, and will dwell in the midst of Jerusalem" (Zech 8:3). The security and peace that God's people will experience come from God's presence in their midst. Peoples and nations of every language will seek God's presence in Jerusalem, taking hold of the garments of the Jews and saying, "Let us go with you, for we have heard that God is with you" (Zech 8:23). And on that day, God will reign from Jerusalem "and the Lord will become king over all the earth" (Zech 14:9).

Israel's prophets project the hope that the departure of God's presence from Jerusalem was temporary and that the transformation of the city will go far beyond a mere restoration of the city to its glory before the exile. But when the temple was constructed again and the walls of Jerusalem rebuilt, they failed to reflect the glory of Solomon's temple or the majesty of God's city. The rich variety of images used in the prophets to describe the future dwelling place of God express God's desire that the divine presence should expand beyond Jerusalem to the ends of the earth. Yet the sinfulness of God's people prevents the growth of God's presence and requires that God's glory be experienced through an altogether new temple.

The Church as Sacrament of God's Universal Reign

The gospel proclaims that the kingdom of God is at hand through the life, death, and resurrection of Jesus. He is the temple not made with human hands, the sanctuary destroyed and rebuilt in three days, the manifestation of God's presence on the earth. Through the Holy Spirit, the community of his disciples manifests his risen presence in the world. As this community of witnesses expands from Jerusalem to the ends of the earth, God's palpable presence on the earth expands outward.

As the body of Christ in the world, the church is the new temple of God. Built on the foundation of the apostles and prophets, with Jesus Christ as the cornerstone, "the whole structure is joined together and grows into a holy temple in the Lord" (Eph 2:21). Paul teaches that in Christ, all God's people become one, holy, universal, and apostolic sanctuary for the Lord's indwelling. His prayer that the members of the church "may be filled with all the fullness of God" (Eph 3:19) alludes to the ancient image of the tabernacle and the temple being filled with God's glory.

In writing to the church at Corinth, Paul writes, "We are the temple of the living God; as God said, 'I will live in them and walk among them'" (2 Cor 6:16). He emphasizes that God not only dwells *with* people and *among* them, as the prophets had declared, but God now dwells *in* them. The new temple is Christ's church, with the Holy Spirit living within each member and filling the whole living sanctuary with the divine presence.

Peter's first letter also describes the community of disciples as a living temple, offering sacrifice to God through Jesus Christ:

> *Like living stones, let yourselves be built into a*
> *spiritual house, to be a holy priesthood, to offer*
> *spiritual sacrifices acceptable to God through Jesus*
> *Christ.* {1 PET 2:5}

As a living and growing sanctuary, the temple expands as the church expands. As "a chosen race, a royal priesthood, a holy nation, God's own people" (1 Pet 2:9), the church is destined by God to become a holy temple covering all the earth.

The book of Revelation completes the divine trajectory that began in Genesis, expressing God's desire that the whole world be a divine dwelling and that divine sovereignty be extended over all the earth. From garden, to tabernacle, to temple in Jerusalem, to church, each phase of God's saving plan completes the previous and anticipates the next. The couple in the garden, the priests and kings of Israel, and the members of Christ's church anticipate the royal and priestly people God desires to live in the universal kingdom. Eventually, God will reign over all creation, and the powers of evil will be destroyed. Those who gather around God's throne sing a "new song," proclaiming the royal and priestly character of all who follow Christ: "You have made them to be a kingdom and priests serving our God, and they will reign on earth" (Rev 5:10).

At the completion of salvation history, the new Jerusalem will come forth from heaven, and God's kingdom will be established in all its glory. "A new heaven and a new earth" will be manifested, and "the new Jerusalem" will come down out of heaven from God, prepared to be joined to Christ, as bride to husband. And a voice from God's throne says:

> *"See, the home of God is among mortals.*
> *He will dwell with them;*
> *they will be his peoples,*
> *and God himself will be with them;*
> *he will wipe every tear from their eyes.*
> *Death will be no more;*
> *mourning and crying and pain will be no more,*
> *for the first things have passed away."* [**REV 21:3–4**]

Heaven is joined to earth as God comes to live with humanity. God's reign is established all over the world so that God may dwell with them throughout the earth.

Finding Our Place in the Unfolding Drama

As we have seen, the Bible is essentially one unfolding drama. Set against the backdrop of God's design for creation, and of human rebellion against that design, the Bible is the narrative of God's redemption of the world. Although the Bible consists of a variety of books and types of literature, it is one story of salvation. Patriarchs and matriarchs, prophets, judges, kings, priests, apostles, and evangelists belong to this inspired book of life.

This biblical account of redemption encompasses the whole world and offers us God's intentions and desires, which give meaning and purpose to human life. The one story of salvation invites us into a grand narrative, explaining for us the way things are, how they have come to be so, and what they will ultimately be. It begins with creation and ends with the renewal of all things in the new creation for which we are destined. And in between, it offers us an interpretation of the whole of human history. Learning to take a panoramic view of the Bible enables us to live in the narrative and discover the real story of which each of our lives is a part.

The biblical scholar N.T. Wright describes the Bible and our role within it with an analogy. He imagines that the script of a lost Shakespearean play is somehow discovered. Although the play originally had five acts, only a little more than four have been found—the first four acts and the first scene of act five. The rest is missing. The play is given to Shakespearean actors who are asked to work out the rest of act five for themselves. Immersing themselves in Shakespearean language and in the narrative of the partial script that has been recovered, they improvise the missing parts of the fifth act, allowing their performance to be shaped by the trajectory of the story as they have come to understand it. In this way they bring the play toward the conclusion that its author had indicated previously in the play.

Wright says that this analogy may help us to understand how the Bible can shape our own lives now. The biblical drama of redemption unfolds in five acts: 1) creation, 2) the fall into sin, 3) Israel's story, 4) the story of Jesus Christ, and 5) the story of the church, leading to the consummation of God's plan of redemption. We know that the Author of the drama, the Divine "Playwright," has given the gift of his own Spirit to the "actors." So we must live our lives within the trajectory of the story as it has been told up to the first part of the final act. We have been entrusted to perform the continuation of the biblical drama within the mission of Jesus and his church, moving the story forward to the conclusion that God has already imagined.[1]

This unfinished drama of salvation, containing its own plot, impetus, and motion, demands that those who enter it bring it to a satisfactory conclusion. We are invited to freely and responsibly enter into the plot as it stands, continually poring over and immersing ourselves in the earlier acts, and learning to understand how the threads can be drawn together. We then improvise, speaking and acting creatively, yet in a way consistent with the story of Israel, Jesus, and the early church. We each imaginatively yet faithfully live out the narrative impetus given in Scripture in the new historical and cultural situations in which our lives are placed by God.

The Bible is indeed a wonderful library of seventy-three books. But all of this wonderful variety of books forms one tradition and is encompassed in one Bible. This essential library of the descendants of Abraham is the book of the church. When we understand that the Bible is our literature, we cross over the threshold and enter into the story ourselves, and we view our lives as participants in the grand narrative of salvation. The more that we can understand the whole Bible as the one great drama of salvation, from creation to new creation, and then find ourselves within that great story, the better we will embody Scripture and become participants in the mission of God.

❖ ❖ ❖

KEYS FOR UNLOCKING THE DOOR

The creation and new creation, from Genesis to Revelation, form a framework for the entire Bible.

The Bible expresses God's desire that the world should become a dwelling place shared by God, humanity, and the creatures of the earth.

God's dwelling in the tabernacle and the temple of Jerusalem are the early stages of God's plan to make the whole earth the divine dwelling.

In the midst of destruction and loss, the prophets gave hope to God's people by proclaiming a new temple, a new Jerusalem, and a new creation.

The writings of Paul and Peter show that the church is the new temple for God's indwelling.

From garden, to tabernacle, to temple in Jerusalem, to church, each phase of God's saving plan completes the previous and anticipates the next phase of God's plan for the priestly kingdom.

The grand narrative of the world's salvation told throughout the Bible offers cohesion, purpose, and meaning for our lives.

❖ ❖ ❖

QUESTIONS FOR REFLECTION AT THE THRESHOLD

- Why is it essential that every book of the Bible be interpreted within the context of all the others?

- What indicates in the opening chapters of Genesis that God desires people to enjoy a royal and priestly status?

- In what sense does God dwell on earth in the tabernacle and the temple?

- In what ways do the words of Isaiah, Ezekiel, and Zechariah give me hope for the future?

- What are the implications for the church as Paul describes it as God's temple built on the prophets of Israel and the apostles of Jesus?

- What are the characteristics of the new Jerusalem emphasized by the book of Revelation?

- In what ways can studying Scripture help me to enter into the plot and find my place in the unfinished drama?

❖ ❖ ❖

PRAYER FOR CROSSING THE THRESHOLD

God of all creation, you desire the whole world to be your dwelling place and the location of your reign. Teach me my dignity as your royal representative and lead me to find my place in the drama of your unfolding plan. May your kingdom come and your will be done, so that all people recognize and join your mission for the world's redemption.

Crossing the Threshold...

6 From Literalism to Fuller Meaning

IN ORDER TO READ THE BIBLE AT A DEEPER LEVEL AS GOD'S WORD, WE MUST MOVE FROM A LITERALIST TO A CONTEXTUAL- IST INTERPRETATION. The literalist reads the text merely on the surface. The meaning of the passage is what it seems to say when looking only superficially at the words themselves. The literal- istic reader reads without a sufficient awareness of metaphor, symbolism, genre, literary style, and so on. The contextualist, in contrast, knows that the text must always be read in its context— that is, taking into account all the circumstances surrounding the passage that can affect its meaning. The contextual reader of Scripture examines the literary, historical, and theological context in order to understand the meaning more fully.

The need to move from a literalist to a contextualist inter- pretation applies to the literature of any culture. We might compare the way children and adults read *The Chronicles of Narnia*, by C.S. Lewis. Children read the novels as enchant- ing stories in which they cross the threshold of the wardrobe into a magical world in which they are invited to participate.

Adults, too, are drawn into the enchanted world of Narnia, but they become more deeply aware of the ways the author uses metaphor to teach. Adults are more able to explore the symbolism and understand the genre through which Lewis expresses profound truths about the meaning of human life.

Stepping into the Fuller Meaning of Jonah

By comparing a literalist reading of the book of Jonah with that of a contextualist, we can better understand the importance of crossing over the threshold into a fuller, contextual understanding of biblical texts. For the literalist, as for the child, the account of Jonah is an amazing tale of a prophet who flees from God in a ship, is thrown overboard, and gets swallowed by a gigantic fish for three days and nights. By looking only at the words on the surface of the text, the literalist can enjoy the story, but fails to comprehend the deeper meaning that the author wants to express in this biblical text.

Jonah is one of the least understood books of the Bible because its meaning is so often lost amid discussions raised by literalists over whether or not the story actually happened. Whether or not a person could survive for three days and nights inside a giant sea creature really misses the point. There may very well have been a prophet of Israel named Jonah, but this tale is clearly not meant to be his biography. The literary devices of humor, irony, exaggeration, and sarcasm used by the author show that the story of Jonah is a satire. This form of literature was common in the ancient world, as it is today, to expose people's vices, follies, abuses, and shortcomings by holding them up to ridicule. It is usually a form of social criticism to draw attention to important issues in society. Let's take a look at how the tale of Jonah does just that.

Jonah is called by God to go to Nineveh, the ancient capital of Assyria, to proclaim God's judgment for their wickedness. The city of Nineveh represents the hated foreigners, or Gentiles. Disobeying God's command, Jonah boards a ship bound for Tarshish, far to the west of Israel, rather than going to Nineveh, far to the east. Clearly, Jonah is trying to run away from God's will. In fact, this prophet, whom the reader would expect to be God's closest servant, is the only character in this whole story filled with Gentiles who fails to obey God. The writer paints Jonah as a foolish, even delusional character who is blinded to the folly of his own deeds.

God casts a great storm upon the sea, and the ship is in danger of breaking up. All the foreign mariners pray, while Jonah the Israelite sleeps obliviously in the ship's hold. The sailors know that the storm is a divine response to something that someone aboard has done. Casting lots to discern who is responsible, the lot falls on Jonah. When Jonah is questioned by the crew, he arrogantly boasts that he is a Hebrew and that his God is the Lord, who made the sea and the dry land. The mariners are even more afraid now. They are reluctant to harm Jonah and do everything possible to row the ship to shore. But as a last resort, after praying to God not to hold them accountable for Jonah's life, they throw him overboard; and the sea immediately becomes calm. Converted to Israel's God, these foreign sailors offer sacrifice and show themselves as model believers, fearing God and offering prayers and sacrificial offerings.

Jonah is then swallowed by a great fish and travels in its belly for three days and nights. Whether such a thing is actually possible is irrelevant. The whole story is intended to be as exaggerated and preposterous as possible because its very purpose is to make fun of Jonah and his attitude. Trapped inside the fish, Jonah finally prays. But his prayer is a psalm of thanksgiving, which is totally inappropriate to his situation, although it is totally appropriate for a reader reflecting on the real message of the book. There is no indication that Jonah is repentant or regrets his disobedience. Then, after three days, the almighty God speaks to the fish and tells it what to do. In a comic twist, the fish vomits the distasteful prophet out upon the dry land.

A second time, God tells Jonah to go to Nineveh, and this time the prophet reluctantly goes. The size of the city is exaggerated beyond any semblance of reality, and Jonah utters only a brief oracle—"Forty days more, and Nineveh shall be overthrown"—then he turns and abruptly leaves. Unlike other prophets, who cry out repeatedly with vivid language and metaphors, Jonah does not want his audience to listen. He wants these hated Ninevites to ignore his message so that God will destroy them. Instead, every citizen of Nineveh, from the greatest to the least important, turns to God. The king orders all the people and animals to fast, put on sackcloth, repent, and pray. The humorous scene of the cattle, goats, and sheep all dressed in sackcloth and crying out to God emphasizes the satirical purpose of the story and helps drive home the point.

The final scene shows Jonah infuriated with God for being so merciful. In a last attempt to teach Jonah a lesson, God causes a bush to grow to give Jonah shade, and Jonah's anger turns to happiness. But the next day God causes the bush to wither and Jonah returns to his misery. And the tale of Jonah ends with a rhetorical question: if Jonah is so concerned about the simple bush, should not God be concerned about the great city of Nineveh and its one hundred and twenty thousand people and its many animals? The question along with the story is intended to teach a lesson to its readers in a colorful, humorous, and memorable way. This satire makes the point that God cares about all of creation, even the lowliest of creatures. The prophet's narrow-minded bigotry toward non-Israelites is what the story satirizes. He embodies an attitude that was present in Israel. Ideally, it helps the readers understand the silliness of their own prejudices and the depths into which their arrogance can lead them.

Only a contextual reading of the book of Jonah leads us to understand the purpose of the book and the truth that the author wishes to express. Knowing the context of the times, the audience addressed, the literary genre of the tale, and its place within the literature of the Old Testament, leads us to interpret the book with insight and avoid a simplistic or superficial reading.

Interpreting the Bible Contextually

To interpret the words of Scripture authentically and reliably, we must always consider the context in which particular texts are situated. Here are some of the major considerations for this kind of interpretation:[1]

1) Interpret in light of the historical and cultural background. An immense historical and cultural gap divides the world of the Bible and the world of the modern-day reader. Just as it would be difficult for Ezekiel or Paul to enter the twenty-first century and understand our world, it is challenging to try to enter the world of the biblical authors. Yet learning something of the setting, situation, and customs of biblical times can help us immensely when interpreting the Scriptures. If we knew nothing about the Samaritans, for instance, we would read the parable of the good samaritan (Lk 10:25–37) simply as a story about a good person who helps another person in need. It would be a good lesson, but not the radical teaching Jesus intended it to be. When we understand that the Samaritans were despised as foreigners and heretics by the Jewish people, the parable becomes a sweeping support for universal justice and love of the outcast.

2) Interpret in light of the author's purpose. The meaning intended by the original biblical author is the foundational meaning of any passage, so we must always try to understand the passage first from the author's point of view. Often authors will give hints as to the purpose of their writing within the book itself. At the end of John's gospel, for example, the evangelist states his intention in writing the gospel: "These are written so that you may come to believe that Jesus is the Messiah, the Son of God, and that through believing you may have life in his name" (John 20:31). He wrote in order to enhance the faith of his readers in Jesus as the Messiah and Son of God, not to give us a detailed and precise biography of Jesus. By keeping John's purpose in mind, we will not be too concerned with why the order and details of John's gospel are so different than that of the other three gospels.

3) Interpret in light of the literary type. As an anthology of religious literature, the Bible contains epic history, poetry, laws, parables, prayers, symbolic visions, songs, and proverbs. The Bible contains all the rich diversity we would expect of a religious culture that spanned nearly two thousand years, from the life of Abraham to the apostolic church. Understanding the type of writing we are reading when we study any part of the Bible can carry us far in understanding the type of truth and religious message contained in the text. For example, we cannot begin to interpret the book of Revelation unless we know that it is apocalyptic writing, a literary type that is written in situations of crisis. Knowing that this type of literature is filled with symbolic and mysterious imagery, we can come to understand that Revelation is not a factual forecast of the future, but a hopeful view of God's conquest of sin and death in the midst of trials and persecution.

4) Interpret in light of the literary context. By reading a passage along with its surrounding verses and within the context of the entire book, we will be led to understand it better and not force a meaning opposed to the intention of its author. For example, many throughout history have taken Paul's words, "Slaves, obey your earthly masters with fear and trembling" (Eph 6:5), as biblical justification for slavery. But those words must be interpreted within the context of that passage, which is discussing how people in all relationships should be mutually submissive toward one another (Eph 5:21). When read in the context of Paul's writings about the freedom the gospel provides, we understand that Paul was not promoting the institution of slavery, but was promoting radically new relationships within the accepted institutions of the time.

5) Interpret in light of the canon of Scripture. The biblical texts take on fuller meaning when read in the context of the whole Bible. So, when we read a violent text of Scripture that doesn't sound like it should be coming from the merciful God we have come to know, we realize that every Scripture passage is only a small part of the whole. When the people of Israel exact a destructive and vengeful conquest of their enemies in pursuit of what seems to be the direction of God, we can read that passage in the context of God's further revelation in Jonah and the other prophets, which speaks of God's merciful concern for all people.

6) Interpret in light of human reason and experience. Rational thinking and sensible experience form a kind of lens through which we view and interpret the Bible. So philosophy and social sciences can be important auxiliary fields to biblical studies to aid understanding. For instance, if an ancient precept in the Bible seems to contradict the norms of universal ethics, it would be important to explore the purpose of that law in its context rather than simply apply it to contemporary practice.

The norms of reason and experience can help us establish a rational and consistent approach to rightly interpreting and correctly understanding the teachings of Scripture.

7) Interpret in light of the ongoing tradition of the community. The history of Israel and of the church is the living tradition in which the books of the Bible were written, and it is the ongoing Jewish and Christian tradition in which these writings continue to be interpreted. We read in the light of the believing communities that have continued to understand new meanings within the text in every age. The Talmud of Judaism and the patristic writers of Christianity, for example, are an important matrix in which to interpret biblical texts. This tradition of the synagogue and the church is the ongoing life, teaching, prayer, worship, scholarship, and theological reflection of each community.

Seeking Fuller Meaning in the Bible

Part of what makes studying the Bible so fascinating is the discovery of rich layers of meaning in each passage. Biblical texts offer continually fuller meaning to each person and each generation. Because the Bible is a living text, no passage of Scripture can be fully explained by a single meaning. For this reason, studying the Bible can never be complete.

To understand how biblical passages reveal deepening layers of meaning, it is helpful to distinguish between what a text meant when it was written and what it means today. The original meaning of a text—what it meant to the human author and its first audience in their historical context—is the foundational meaning of any passage. This original meaning contains an essential and foundational truth. All other meanings discovered within a text must be rooted in and built upon this foundation.

In addition to the original meaning, biblical texts contain fuller meanings that could not have been understood by their original authors. This is a characteristic of any classical work of literature being read at a later period and in a different context, but it is particularly true of the Bible because these books are the foundational literature of living traditions. When these writings were joined into the compilation called the Bible, this collection itself formed connections between the texts that no author could have foreseen, enlarging the meaning originally intended.

The patristic writers of the church's early centuries considered their interpretation of biblical texts complete only when they had found a meaning pertinent and applicable to the situation of Christians in their own day. Their understanding of the Bible's inspiration assured them, as it assures the church today, that the biblical texts have vital meaning for all times and contain eternal truths for all people. This ongoing encounter over the centuries between the sacred texts and the community of faith uncovers meaning in biblical passages beyond what the original authors could have envisioned in their limited circumstances and adds fuller meaning to the original sense of the text.

The following are a few different types of fuller meaning that can be discovered in biblical texts:

The messianic meaning. In the later centuries of ancient Israel, following the destruction of Jerusalem and the Babylonian exile, scholars and scribes began to look at the promises of the covenant and the oracles of the prophets in a new light. Since the monarchy had ended and many of God's assurances about the house of King David remained incompletely fulfilled, they began to anticipate a completion of God's work in the future age of the Messiah. This new meaning of ancient texts does not replace the original meaning, but enriches it with fuller implications and hopeful meaning.

For Christian believers, the life, death, and resurrection of Jesus established a radically new historical context for all the texts of the ancient covenant. The new covenant in him shed fresh light on the Old Testament writings and brought them fuller meaning. This Christological sense of the texts of Israel is the fuller meaning discerned when they are read in the context of the paschal mystery of Christ and guided by his Spirit. It always demonstrates a profound conformity with the text's original meaning, while, at the same time, giving it a fuller meaning. The new meaning does not replace the foundational meaning of the Old Testament text, but remains in continuity with it, retaining its original meaning while expressing its inspired fullness.

The Acts of the Apostles expresses this fuller, messianic meaning in its description of the encounter between Philip and the Ethiopian court official along the road leading from Jerusalem. When Philip sees the Ethiopian in his chariot reading from the prophet Isaiah, Philip asks the man if he understands what he is reading. And the Ethiopian admits that he needs some help. He invites Philip into his chariot and asks him about whom the prophet is speaking. The text from Acts continues, "Then Philip began to speak, and starting with this scripture, he proclaimed to him the good news about Jesus" (Acts 8:35). This passage from the prophet Isaiah, Philip explains, has a richer and fuller meaning in the light of the coming of Christ than could have been understood by the original writer. Although Isaiah's words may have made sense to his Israelite hearers in their historical context, their meaning is most complete in the light of Christ. We see this same pattern throughout Acts, especially in the speeches of Peter and Paul. They quote continually from the Old Testament to proclaim how Jesus is the climax of God's saving plan for the world.

The canonical meaning. Although each biblical book and passages within those books have their own independent meanings, these texts take on fuller meaning as they are understood within the context of the whole Bible. Individual Hebrew texts achieved fuller meaning when read in the context of the Jewish Torah, prophets, and writings (Tanak). Older texts were often quoted in new contexts, giving those texts a new and enlarged significance. This fuller meaning of Old Testament texts was often expressed by New Testament writers. Through quotations and references, they demonstrated how the ancient texts pointed to the new covenant.

One way in which this canonical meaning is expressed is through what is called the "typical sense." This is the deeper meaning of persons, places, and events in the Bible when they are understood as foreshadowing future aspects of God's work of salvation. The "type" is a shadow or silhouette of the future reality. For example, the passage of Jonah in the belly of the fish is a type of Jesus' stay in the tomb (Matt 12:40–41); the Passover lamb of Exodus is a type of the sacrifice of Christ (John 1:29); the passage of Israel through the sea is a type of Christian baptism (1 Cor 10:2). God's saving plan is characterized by a pattern of promise and fulfillment in which God's future realization is prepared through past revelation.

The communal meaning. The Bible developed within the ancient traditions of Israel and the apostolic church, and the faith of these communities found expression in its texts. These sacred texts have shaped the development and renewal of these living communities in the synagogue and the church through the ages. The communal meaning of a biblical text is the fuller meaning of that text as it is understood in light of the ongoing experience of these active communities. After the biblical text has left the hands of its original author, the dialogue between the text and the believing community through time unfolds the text's fuller meaning.

The book of Jonah was a reminder to the community of

Israel that God loves all the people of the world, and it challenged their exclusivist attitudes. For the church, the book reinforces Jesus' teachings on love of enemies, and it urges the church outward to the fringes, in mission to all people.

Because of this living, communal tradition, the act of interpreting is open-ended, and no single interpretation of a text can claim to be the final, once-and-for-all meaning. The ultimate question of meaning is not simply, "What does the text mean?" as if the words have some abstract and isolated meaning, but "What is the meaning of the text for the believing community?" Understanding the Bible as divine revelation presumes a community that receives and responds to God's word.

The challenge of determining fuller meanings in a text beyond the original meaning is ongoing. The interpreter must always consider whether a further interpretation is legitimate or not, whether or not it is an organic development from the original meaning. We all know that the Bible can be made to say many things that cannot be justified by a contextual reading. We must make sure that our work of interpretation is truly "exegesis" (that is, discovering meaning in the text itself) and not "eisegesis" (that is, imposing a meaning upon a text that cannot be found in the text itself). Genuine and faithful interpretation of Scripture is a constant and essential challenge for scholars, pastors, and all people who read Scripture as the word of God.

❖ ❖ ❖

KEYS FOR UNLOCKING THE DOOR

 Crossing the threshold from a literalist to a contextualist interpretation is necessary for reading Scripture as God's word.

🗝 Knowing the historical context, the audience addressed, the author's intention, and the literary type helps avoid superficial and misguided interpretations of biblical passages.

🗝 Since the Bible is God's living word, we can always discover new insights and deeper levels of meaning in each text.

🗝 When the ancient literature of Israel became part of the complete Bible and became part of the church's ongoing tradition, these texts gained fuller meanings that the original authors could not have anticipated.

🗝 The "typical sense" is the deeper meaning that some persons, places, and events of the Bible have because God intended that these elements foreshadow further aspects of God's work of salvation.

🗝 The communal meaning of a biblical text is the fuller meaning of that text as it is understood in light of the ongoing experience and tradition of Israel and the church.

🗝 To avoid misguided interpretation, we must always consider whether or not a fuller meaning is legitimately rooted in the original meaning and builds upon it.

❖ ❖ ❖

QUESTIONS FOR REFLECTION AT THE THRESHOLD

● After reading the short story of Jonah, does it seem more likely that the book is an ancient novel or an eyewitness narrative? In what ways is the story of Jonah like a parable?

- How does God communicate divine truth through fictional stories? How does Jesus communicate truth through the fiction of his parables?

- Some people approach the Bible with this attitude: "God said it, I believe it, end of discussion." What are some of the pitfalls of this approach to interpreting Scripture?

- Which of the major considerations for interpreting the Bible contextually seem most important?

- Why is the typical sense of a person, place, or event of Scripture not part of the original meaning of the text? Give an example or two.

- What is the importance of "exegesis" for interpreting a text? What is the danger of "eisegesis" in the work of interpretation?

- What are some ways I might be able to discern whether or not a biblical interpretation is valid and not totally subjective?

PRAYER FOR CROSSING THE THRESHOLD

Saving God, you sent your Son, the divine Word, to be incarnate in our world so that your people might experience your life within their own. You gave us the inspired Scriptures through human authors and human language so that we might experience your revelation in ways we can understand. Help me to always discover deeper levels of meaning in your living word.

Crossing the Threshold...

7 From Information to Transformation

THE CULTURE IN WHICH WE LIVE TODAY IS CHARACTERIZED BY A DESIRE TO KNOW MORE AND TO DO MORE. Certainly there is nothing wrong with this orientation in itself, but a pervasively informational way of knowing more, and a mostly functional way of doing more, can significantly narrow the experience of life. An excessive emphasis on information and functioning can prevent us from attaining the wholeness that God desires for us.

In seeking more information, we become consumed with new facts, new techniques and programs, new methods and systems. Our digital age has accelerated this obsession with information exponentially. Our consumer culture combined with our acquisitive nature convinces us that the more we know, the better off we are. Those with the most and the best information are able to control others and their environment.

This informational and functional orientation today clearly affects the way we read. We try to read as much as possible and as quickly as possible. Powerful internet search engines present us with more information about any subject than we could possibly consume. Our daily scan of news media, social media, blogs, and trending stories requires an increasingly large part of our time. When we read for information, we are reading with some functional purpose. We want to control the text so that we can use it for our own purposes. We read to increase our knowledge of a topic so we can master it. Or we read critically so that we can impose our own opinion on the text. Or we read to solve problems, always trying to make our lives and the things around us run to our satisfaction.

Reading Scripture, whether we realize it or not, is deeply affected by this desire to know more and to do more. The informational and functional way of reading influences our motivation for reading the Bible. We might read with a rapid-reading plan so as to have a comprehensive knowledge of the Bible. Or we peruse the Bible looking for advice, so that we can fix the confusion or dysfunction we might be experiencing in life. Or we read so that we can teach our children, or discuss with our friends, or defend ourselves against the challenges of fundamentalists or non-believers.

Of course, there is nothing wrong with any of these reasons or motivations for reading Scripture. Seeking information must always be a part of our reading. But allowing the informational and functional approaches to dominate prevents us from experiencing the transformational purpose of God's word. Informational reading only gets us to the front porch. Opening the door and crossing the threshold requires a different mode of reading and listening to God's word.

Formational Reading of Scripture
Reading the Bible for information is certainly necessary because God's revelation has an essential cognitive dimension.

But the intellectual aspects of Scripture are only one dimension of the inspired word through which God wants to free us and make us whole. Although there are lots of good reasons for reading the Bible, the best reason is to be formed into the image of Jesus Christ.

Rather than keeping Scripture at a safe and analytical distance and under our control, this formational reading leads to our encounter with God's word. We open ourselves to personal engagement with God through Scripture. We involve ourselves intimately, openly, and receptively in what we read.

Formational reading does not aim at reading as much as possible and as quickly as possible. The concern, rather, is with the quality of reading. Its goal is not to control or use the text to get advice or solve a problem. We don't read with a practical purpose, nor do we read with the aim of forming an opinion about the text. We don't use Scripture to do more, but to improve the quality of our being.

Reading Scripture in this way not only lets us discover multiple layers of meaning in the text, but it allows the text to probe deeper levels of our own being. Rather than treating the text as an object that we control, the inspired text becomes the subject of the reading relationship. We become the object that is acted upon and shaped by Scripture. We remain patiently and receptively with the text, waiting for the divine word to address us, to probe us, and to form us.

Allowing Scripture to form us requires humility and receptivity. We must relinquish our acquisitive desire to know more and to do more, and we must await the formative work of God's Spirit. We remain open to the mystery of God's revelation through the Spirit-breathed text, and we stay ready to be addressed by God.

This formational mode of reading Scripture is a discipline that must be developed. We can't just pick up the Bible and start reading like we would a magazine. It requires preparation. We have to silence ourselves, letting go of our lives and trusting in the presence of God. Then we can take up the sacred book and listen to the word address us. As we get into the habit of preparing ourselves for formational reading, we gradually become more open to God's presence in other areas of our lives. We begin to live more receptively and more responsively to God in our daily lives.

Putting on the Mind and Heart of Jesus Christ

God desires to free us from bondage and to form us into the image of Christ. This is the heart of the Christian life and the primary goal of reading Scripture. Through faith and baptism we live a new life, a life "in Christ." This new life involves a new way of seeing, a new way of being, a new way of living—indeed, a new identity. To be "in Christ" means to live as a "new creation" (2 Cor 5:17).

When Paul urges his listeners to live the Christian life, he writes, "Let the same mind be in you that was in Christ Jesus" (Phil 2:5). He wants them to be formed in such a way that they can truly say, "We have the mind of Christ" (1 Cor 2:16). Putting on the mind of Christ means taking on his way of thinking, his freedom, his approach to life. This is the formation that God wants to create within us through his word.

When we read the Old Testament narratives, for example, we listen to the stories of Israel's ancestors that formed the mind-set of Jesus. When we read the psalms, we are hearing the prayers that formed the heart of Jesus, the chants of the temple and synagogue that formed Jesus' prayers to the Father. When we read the prophets, we hear the words that molded Jesus' understanding of his own mission to God's people. Thus, absorbing our minds in the Old Testament shapes our attitudes and understandings to be like that of Christ.

Likewise, formational reading of the four gospels, the Acts of the Apostles, and the letters of the New Testament forms us to take on the mind and heart of Christ. When we imagine his saving deeds, listen to his teachings, and read about the work of his Holy Spirit in the lives of his followers, we fill our own imaginations with the words, images, and vision of life that filled the mind of Jesus.

Formative reading of Scripture means growing to live in Christ and putting on his mind and heart. Our minds and hearts work together to create images and concepts that we can't tangibly experience with our five senses. Actually, what the five senses are to our physical bodies, the imagination is to our embodied spirit. It is the gateway to spiritual experiences that are more real than what we can experience only in the material world.

There has been an unfortunate de-emphasis on the important role of the imagination in the past couple of centuries. Our rationalistic world has convinced us that anything we might experience in our imagination is just fanciful and unreal. Yet God speaks to us in our imaginations, and through our imaginations we open ourselves more fully to the spiritual reality of God's life and promises. When we engage our imagination, the senses of the soul, we open ourselves to be formed by Scripture. With our minds and hearts engaged, we submit our imagination to the work of God's Spirit, and we gradually become formed into the new life of Christ.

When we read Isaiah, for instance, we imagine Isaiah's vision in the temple and hear the seraphim calling out: "Holy, holy, holy is the Lord of hosts; the whole earth is full of his glory" (Isa 6:3). And when these images present themselves to our soul, we begin to catch more glimpses of God's glory reflected in the tangible experiences of life—in the sunrise, the waterfall, and the eagle's flight. We realize that the whole earth is charged with God's grandeur. Then we continue reading Isaiah and find an extraordinary vision of a world healed by God's love, a world in which the wolf and the lamb lie together in peace, a world of reconciliation and harmony, where the swords for making war are transformed to plowshares for making peace. So with a soul filled with hope, we know that we must live between this world filled with reflections of God's glory and a future in which all that disfigures God's design is done away with and the glorious presence of God renews the whole creation.

When we read the biblical prophets, we realize that they did not despair amidst the idolatry and injustice around them. Rather, they called people to hope. Their continual refrain was "The day is coming," a day when God will rule, injustice will cease, evil will be made right, and God's people will experience the deliverance for which they have hoped. Their message required that their hearers in Israel form images and concepts in their imaginations contrary to what they experienced with their senses. The prophets formed God's people in hope and shaped their imaginations with the truths and promises that God revealed.

Reading the gospels, we realize that Jesus calls his followers to an even greater act of imagination. While the prophets promised that "the day is coming," Jesus proclaims that "the day has come." The day the prophets envisioned has come upon us. Jesus taught that the kingdom of God is at hand, and he told parables to express what the kingdom is like. He filled the imaginations of his disciples, enabling them to see the reality of God's reign in the world beneath the appearances of human experience.

When the scribe asked Jesus what he must do to receive eternal life, Jesus asked him about the commandments of the law. The scribe answered correctly when he repeated the two great commands—to love God and neighbor. Although he tried to trap Jesus with a technical question, "Who is my neighbor?" Jesus replied with a story in order to drive the question beyond the intellectual realm and into the heart. With the unforgettable parable of the good samaritan, Jesus enriched the scribe's imagination and that of his whole church. Jesus was not just concerned that his followers know his teachings, but that they actually follow in his way. His final words were "Go and do likewise" (Luke 10:37).

God forms us through Scripture by filling our lives with supernatural imagery and inspired revelation. Through the Bible, God helps us understand that truth is not limited to what we can perceive with the senses. In this way, God frees our minds, enlarges our perspectives, and broadens our horizons. An imagination nourished with Scripture knows that incarnation and resurrection are real and that divine life is our destiny. It enables us to live within the great story of salvation, a grand vision of reality, from creation to the new creation when God will bring earth and heaven together finally and forever.

In this world today, with all its present ugliness and pain, the word of God calls us to put on the mind and heart of Christ, to embody his gospel, and to be agents of the new creation. We can live as his disciples because we know that the kingdom of God is upon us and the new creation has broken into our world with healing and redemption. The formative word of God enables us to inhabit a world where God reigns, where evil has been conquered, where sinners have been redeemed, and where Christ is seated at God's right hand in glory.

As we learn to read Scripture formatively, we come to the Bible like an Orthodox worshiper approaches an icon. The believer looks at the icon from the outside and is drawn into it. The faces, gestures, movements, and colors invite the believer to step into a fuller reality than our material world. Contemplating with an icon is an experience of being drawn into the kingdom of heaven where Christ and the saints dwell, where the saving deeds of Christ are received by the Father, and where the saving mysteries of the faith are eternal.

Reading Scripture formatively is a very similar experience. The inspired text draws us in. The characters and the scenes capture our imaginations and invite us into their world. Through the Holy Spirit alive in the text and within us, the Scriptures breathe God's truth, goodness, and beauty. As God's living word, the Scriptures captivate us and move us toward God's grace so that we might share in the divine life. They form us from lost and sinful creatures of the earth into saved and immortal creatures who will live forever in God.

The Bible is not just a collection of uplifting verses to help us feel better. It is more than a manual of solutions to help us fix our problems. It is the living word of God. The more we open our minds and hearts to it, the more it brings us into the presence of God, the more it frees us and transforms us into the image of Christ.

Allowing God's Word to Transform Us

The whole Bible, from beginning to end, proclaims God's grace to the world. God draws near to us while we are still sinners and delights in us. From Genesis to Revelation, the Scriptures speak of God's passionate yearning for us, and they inspire within us a yearning to be in the divine presence. And in this way, the words of the Bible open us to the healing and transforming power of God's grace.

We don't have to earn or deserve this love of God or the transforming power it offers us. God's transforming grace is a divine gift that we must only accept into our lives. We only have to create the necessary conditions within ourselves so that we can receive God's transforming presence. Here are some of the necessary dispositions for allowing God's word to transform us:

Reverence. When we begin reading Scripture, we are entering the mystery of God. God's word is always something more than we can comprehend, and we should never approach it with anything less than veneration and respect. This disposition of reverence before the mystery of God's word instills humility within us. St. Augustine describes his initial arrogance before God: "Proud as I was, I dared to seek that which only the humble can find."[1] We must accept our profound ignorance with regard to God. Filled with hunger and thirst, yearning and need, we know that we can only listen and receive the divine word. When we reverently open the sacred text, we open our hearts to be formed by God.

Openheartedness. We can receive the grace of God's word when we approach it with an open mind and heart. There is much within Scripture that may confuse, frustrate, and even shock us and might even cause us to reject it. But when we open ourselves to be formed by it, God gradually opens the door of our lives and gives us the freedom to be completely dedicated to this gift of grace. On our part, this means ridding ourselves of whatever external attractions and internal passions may be forming obstacles to God's grace. This purgation creates purity of heart and that full receptivity that enables us to be progressively transformed by God's word.

Expectation. To receive God's transforming word, we must trust that God is present and speaks to us through the inspired word, that God desires us and creates a longing for the divine presence within us. This kind of personal trust in a God who cares about us deeply leads us to fully expect to encounter God in the inspired word, to expect God to reveal the divine presence and wisdom as we read. This expectation leads us to read the Bible with empty hands, placing the control in God's hands rather than in our own. Reading with expectation means truly listening, knowing that God's agenda may be different from ours. It means learning how to read the Bible in a way that doesn't require that we have all the answers, but that requires us to stay present to the text as it makes us present to the great mystery of God. It is this trusting expectation that creates the listening ear, the open hands, and the receptive heart that are so necessary to receive God's word in Scripture. When we desire God and are ready for God's presence, we will read Scripture with expectation, and God's word will invite us into a transforming relationship.

Faithfulness. Transformation through God's word is a gradual process. It takes time, dedication, and persistence for reading Scripture to saturate our minds and hearts, our spirits and imaginations, with the words, images, and memories of God's word. Spasmodic bursts of devotion will not work. The more we get to know God through our reading of Scripture, the more we grow in love. Faithfulness to this communication with our divine Lover creates an ever-deepening intimacy. And as we come to know God, the better we grow to know and understand ourselves, for we begin to see ourselves through the eyes of God. This faithful practice of reading Scripture gradually transforms us into the image of God, into the mind and heart of Christ.

KEYS FOR UNLOCKING THE DOOR

 An excessive emphasis on the informational way of knowing more and the functional way of doing more can obstruct the freedom and life that God desires for us.

- Formational reading of Scripture leads to a personal and receptive encounter with God's self-revelation.

- The primary purpose of reading Scripture is to free our lives so that God can form us into the image of Christ.

- Jesus filled the imaginations of his disciples with images and parables to help them experience the reign of God in the midst of the world.

- Gazing on an icon and meditating on the Scriptures are similar experiences in which God invites us into the supernatural reality of God's kingdom.

- Reverence, openheartedness, expectation, and faithfulness are some of the necessary dispositions for allowing God's word to transform us.

- As with any relationship, faithfulness in our communication with God creates an ever-deepening intimacy with God.

❖ ❖ ❖

QUESTIONS FOR REFLECTION AT THE THRESHOLD

- How does the need to know more and to do more influence the way I read the Bible?

- How might a move from informational to formational reading affect my experience of God's word?

- How can I take on "the mind of Christ" and live in him through reading the Old Testament?

● How can reading Scripture with my imagination engaged help in my Christian formation?

● What experiences have helped me to experience my life as a new creation?

● What can I do to approach my reading of Scripture with greater reverence?

● What does it mean to me to read the Bible with expectation?

PRAYER FOR CROSSING THE THRESHOLD

Eternal God, you reveal yourself through your holy word.

As I read the sacred Scriptures, guide me with your Spirit so that I may be formed into the image of Jesus Christ, the divine Word made flesh. Transform me with your grace as I listen to your word with reverence, openheartedness, expectation, and faithfulness.

Crossing the Threshold...

8 From Distraction to Deep Listening

THE HUMAN PERSON IS AN EMBODIED SPIRIT. We experience God's revelation with our intellect, will, memory, emotions, senses, imagination, drives, and desires. Reading Scripture as the word of God requires that we bring the entirety of our being to the practice.

In the ancient world, the reading of Scripture was always done aloud. Even when the reading was in private, readers would always move their lips and vocalize the text. In this way, they saw the text with their eyes, pronounced the text with their lips, and heard the text with their ears. In this way, a range of senses is employed in reading Scripture. The spiritual masters taught that the more senses we can involve in our spiritual practices, the more effectively we will experience the divine. For this reason, the use of candles, chimes, incense, and other sensual stimuli can enhance our experience of the sacred text as the word of God.

But more than involving our senses, we should strive to read Scripture as insiders, as participants in the world of the Bible, and not simply as outsiders, looking in from a distance. This means acquiring an experiential knowledge of the text, rather than simply an intellectual understanding. This means allowing the scenes to become real in our imagination. It means allowing the feelings and emotions expressed in the text to interact with our own. This kind of inside reading leads us to enter the world of the text. As a participant in the biblical world, we bring our whole self to the reading, with both our minds and our hearts engaged. The goal of this holistic reading of Scripture is an encounter with God. The experience of reading Scripture as the word of God leads us to a dialogue with God: first we listen to God speak through the word, and then we respond to God as a reply to this encounter.

For example, when we read Scripture we can come to an intellectual knowledge that God loves us, based on the abstract truths that we discover in the text. Yet, although we know with our head that God loves us, sometimes our heart tells us that God just, well, tolerates us. But then we begin to read the biblical narratives from the inside, especially scenes in which Jesus encounters suffering, sinful, struggling people, and we allow the truth of God's love to be experienced in our heart.

When Jesus looks up at Zacchaeus peering at him from the tree limb and says, "I must stay at your house today," the heart of Jesus is longing to encounter Zacchaeus in a way that will transform his life. And indeed, Zacchaeus' life is turned inside out by that encounter because he discovers that his corruption and many failures are no barrier to the love of God that he experiences in Jesus. In actions more than words, Jesus tells Zacchaeus that God yearns for him and longs to be with him. Right now, despite his sins, God is drawing near to him with love. When we soak in narratives like this with our whole self, we can know with our mind and our heart, feel with our emotions and our desires, and truly experience God changing our lives.

Inside Reading through the Holy Spirit

Reading the ancient biblical texts as an insider is possible because the Scriptures are filled with God's Spirit. As a living book, not just a collection of literature inherited from past ages, the sacred pages have life continually breathed into them by the Holy Spirit. Through the Holy Spirit, the words of the Bible can lead us into a personal, formative encounter with God. When we read it as insiders, under the guidance of the Holy Spirit, it will transform our lives.

In writing that the Bible must be read and interpreted "in the light of the same Spirit by whom it was written," St. Jerome implies that the ever-present divine Spirit joins the author and reader to the living word. St. Irenaeus said that the Spirit ensures the Scriptures' perennial youth. The Spirit continues to speak to us with vigor, making the living word of God present to us on every page. The Spirit breathes power and life into the text so that we can truly encounter the living God within the inspired pages.

The first Christians realized that they did not have the human ability to comprehend everything that God had revealed to them in Jesus. But through the work of the Holy Spirit, they experienced ever-deepening insight and understanding. This is the "Spirit of truth" whom Jesus promised them: "He will guide you into all truth" (John 16:13). As disciples of Jesus today, we can trust in this promise and know that the Spirit will continually guide us as we listen to God's word with reverence, openheartedness, expectation, and faithfulness.

Whenever we take up the Bible and before we begin to read, we should always invoke the Holy Spirit in prayer. We can call upon the Holy Spirit to guide us as we read, enabling us to experience the Scriptures as God's living word. We can trust the Holy Spirit to give us inspiration, to breathe within us, just as the divine Spirit breathed in the sacred writers. We can expect God's Spirit to aid our own efforts to comprehend the texts. The Holy Spirit will gradually open our minds and hearts, enlighten our will and imagination, and motivate our drives and desires. Through the Spirit, God will form us into the image of Christ and help us grow in our faith and love.

Consuming God's Word

The word of God contains the potential to nourish our embodied spirits, just as healthful food contains everything necessary to satisfy our bodily hungers and promote our vigorous development. For this reason, we don't just read Scripture; we assimilate it. We take it in, eat it, chew it, digest it, and we get those words flowing through our bloodstream.

The prophet Ezekiel speaks about his vision of God in which the divine being handed him a scroll written on both sides and tells him to eat the scroll.

> *He said to me, O mortal, eat what is offered to you;*
> *eat this scroll, and go, speak to the house of Israel. So I*
> *opened my mouth, and he gave me the scroll to eat. He*
> *said to me, Mortal, eat this scroll that I give you and*
> *fill your stomach with it. Then I ate it; and in my*
> *mouth it was as sweet as honey. He said to me: Mortal,*
> *go to the house of Israel and speak my very words to*
> *them.* {EZEK 3:1–4}

God placed the inspired word into the prophet so that it could become enfleshed in him. God wanted Ezekiel to experience that word with his whole self—his body, mind, heart, will, and spirit—so that he could genuinely proclaim that word to others.

Likewise, God wants us to experience Scripture deeply so that the word may be digested and so nourish our lives. God desires us to assimilate Scripture so that it may become metabolized in works of healing, justice, and forgiveness. By being digested and metabolized into a form that we may use for God's reign in the world, the sacred text is transformed through us with God's grace into witness and service.

St. Bernard of Clairvaux, a twelfth-century Cistercian abbot and Doctor of the Church, spoke about the word of God as food to be consumed by God's people:

> *I store up the word of God as you would food. The word of God is a living bread, the food of the soul. Bread kept in a cupboard can be stolen, eaten by rats, go stale, but once it is eaten none of these misfortunes are to be feared. Store up the Word of God like that, because blessed are those that keep it. Let it sink into your inmost heart and pass into your affections and way of life. Eat plentifully of it and your soul will rejoice. Never forget to eat this bread, lest your heart wither, but feed and strengthen it with so rich and fruitful a food. If you hold onto the Word, the Word will protect you. The Son of God will come to you and his Father also.*[1]

This deep listening and meditating on Scripture has been aptly referred to by the patristic writers as the "chewing" of Scripture's "sweet and nourishing food." Only by slowly chewing this holy food can we savor it, digest it, and absorb it into our whole being. The tradition refers to this chewing as "rumination," a word that originally described the way a cow chews its cud. The animal's slow, repeated chewing to ensure thorough digestion describes the method of unhurriedly repeating a scriptural text with the intention of making it one's own.

A worthwhile way of "feeding" on Scripture is to choose a sentence or phrase of the text that speaks to us personally, then spend time reflecting on it. We can gently repeat it, taking it to heart, and allowing it to interact with our own thoughts, feelings, memories, hopes, and desires. As we repeat the passage slowly, over and over, we will receive new insights and understanding.

Through this unhurried ruminating, God's word will begin to affect us at increasingly deeper levels. And so, without great effort on our part, but by simply allowing the Spirit to act on us, this gentle reflection on Scripture opens the way for an increasingly deeper unity with God in Jesus Christ.

The Sacred Art of *Lectio Divina*

Although the term *lectio divina* (sacred reading) is not found in ecclesial writings until the third century, this practice is our inheritance from the Jewish tradition and is the church's most ancient way of reading Scripture. Jewish teachers taught their disciples to immerse themselves in prayerful reading of the sacred scrolls. Because the text itself is sacred, the ark containing the biblical scrolls is sacred space in the synagogue, with lamps burning around it, proclaiming God's holy presence. And the Jewish people know that they open themselves to that presence of God through reading and meditating on the Torah, prophets, and writings of Scripture.

The term is found extensively in the patristic writings of the third through the fifth centuries, beginning with Origen. St. Jerome urged his hearers to feed the soul each day with *lectio divina*.[1] This practice nourished the fathers and mothers of the desert in these early centuries and then entered the emerging monastic movement. In the West, St. Benedict incorporated *lectio divina* into his Rule for the monastic life.

By the high Middle Ages, unfortunately, this personal reading of Scripture declined in the church, especially outside the monasteries. The Scholastic method of theology became increasingly suspicious of personal experience and the contemplative dimensions of prayer. During this period, a book by a Carthusian monk named Guigo II, entitled *The Monk's Ladder,* described *lectio divina* as four rungs on an ascending ladder on which monks are "lifted up from earth to heaven." Each rung represents an increasingly higher and more difficult "step."[2] The higher rungs are for those who have special graces, and contemplation was identified with extraordinary mystical states, something to be admired by lay people from a safe distance. This systematizing of the tradition represented a striking departure from the more ancient practice, and partly explains why *lectio divina* went out of favor for many centuries in the church. Today, however, *lectio divina* is experiencing a worldwide revival as Christians return to this age-old wisdom in order to experience Scripture in a deeper and more complete way.

There is no single method for the practice of *lectio divina.* It is not a rigid step-by-step system for encountering God in biblical passages. The spiritual masters of the early church never trusted methods of prayer and spiritual practice that were too rigidly defined. They knew that God's Spirit moves differently in each person and that God's inner work within the individual should not be impeded with unyielding rules. So there is no need to anxiously assess our spiritual practice as if we had to correctly follow a technique to achieve some particular target.

The most important thing to keep in mind when practicing *lectio divina* is that it is meant to lead us to a personal encounter with God through the Scriptures. There is no goal other than prayerfully reading Scripture in God's presence with a desire to deepen our heart-to-heart intimacy. In *lectio divina* we let go of our own agenda and gradually open ourselves to what God want us to experience through the inspired text.[4]

Listening with the Ear of the Heart

Reading a biblical text in the tradition of *lectio divina* means approaching our reading reverently and expectantly, trusting that if we do so, the Holy Spirit will connect us to the inspired word in a personal way. We believe that God will speak the inspired word to us through the sacred page. St. Benedict in his monastic *Rule* described this kind of reading as hearing "with the ear of our heart."[5] God speaks and we listen.

The key to this deep listening is reading the biblical text with as little prejudgment as possible, as if we were hearing it for the first time. We can't listen fully to God if we think we already know what the text is going to tell us. Rather, this expectant reading requires that we create a space within ourselves for the new insight and wisdom God wants to give us through the sacred page.

This deep listening requires careful, fully attentive reading, engaging our mind, our imagination, our emotions, and our will. We savor the words of the sacred literature, appreciating the images, envisioning the scene, feeling the sentiments, allowing the words to move from our heads to our hearts. St. Ambrose urged readers to avoid the tendency to read large passages in haste: "We should read not in agitation, but in calm; not hurriedly, but slowly, a few words at a time, pausing in attentive reflection...Then the readers will experience their ability to enkindle the ardor of prayer."[6]

Struggling with a text can be a prayerful and faith-filled process. Seeking to comprehend its meaning is an important part of encountering God there and being changed by that encounter. The Jewish rabbis and the church's patristic theologians show us that there is no clear distinction between studying Scripture and reading it prayerfully. The more we come to understand Scripture with our minds, the more we are capable of being formed by it.

We will be able to probe the fullest meaning of a text the more we comprehend something of its original context—historical, cultural, literary, and religious. When, where, and why was the author writing? Most importantly, how did the writer's faith manifest itself in the text and what kind of faith response does the writer expect from the reader? Seeking to understand the faith dimension of the text helps us transcend the original circumstances in which it was written and allows us to see the lasting significance and validity it has for all of us.

Bible studies and biblical commentaries can be a great help to understanding. Listening to the text with the understanding of the church and with some basic insights of biblical scholarship can assure us that our comprehension is true and faithful. This listening to the text for understanding—with its multiple layers of meaning and rich history of interpretation—forms the foundation on which we can begin to experience its transforming potential.

With reverent, openhearted, expectant, and faithful listening, the words of Scripture become the means of God speaking to us. As God's Spirit guided the human authors to express the truth that God wished to entrust to the Scriptures, God also guides us through that same Spirit as we read the Bible as God's word to us.

Allowing God's Word to Penetrate Our Lives

After hearing a work of music that has moved us, we naturally want to reflect upon it, letting it resound within us. After reading a poem that strikes us deeply, we want to pause in silence to allow it to echo and complete its work within us. This should be our response to reading Scripture. We want to create a space in our heart for God's word to reside. We allow God's word to take root within us, to penetrate the deepest part of our being so that it becomes a part of us.

The more we listen to God's word, the more it seeps into our lives and saturates our thoughts and feelings. St. Ambrose described how this assimilation takes place: "When we drink from sacred Scripture, the life-sap of the eternal Word penetrates the veins of our soul and our inner faculties."[7] The dynamic word of God so penetrates our lives that it truly infuses our mind and heart, and so we begin to embody its truth and its love.

We allow the word of God to become the word of our lives by reflecting on the text, dialoguing with it, and allowing it into the sphere of our own lives. We must listen for what the Scripture passage is saying to us, what it may be offering us, and what it may be demanding of us. This interior understanding of Scripture is always present to us, lying beneath the surface of the Scriptures. Once we grasp this personal and hidden truth with the mind, we must let it descend to the heart where we can assimilate it more deeply. There the difference between the word of God and our own word is less clear; the distinction between Scripture and our own life is less distinct. When we allow the sacred text to penetrate our minds and our hearts, we have begun to truly embody the inspired word.

Engaging Scripture with the Imagination

In his spiritual writings, especially *The Spiritual Exercises*, St. Ignatius of Loyola builds upon the ancient practice of prayerfully reading Scripture and adds some important dimensions and spiritual disciplines. He instructs us to become attentive to the "movements of the soul," a type of personal examination of our current mental, emotional, and spiritual state. This is not done to become self-focused, but rather to become aware of our needs in order to bring them before God while reading and reflecting on Scripture. In bringing these needs before God, we can then listen for God's response through Scripture.

Ignatius then instructs us to engage our imagination in reading Scripture and to place ourselves within the scene, becoming a participant within the story. Creating a picture of the scene with the imagination, we seek to notice the details and consider the five bodily senses: What might we see? What sounds would we hear? We try to imagine the feel of the environment, the smells and tastes we would experience in the scene. As a participant in a gospel scene, we might image ourselves as a disciple, a person being healed, a member of the crowd being taught, or any number of roles. Then we go beneath the senses to our minds and hearts: What am I thinking and feeling at this moment? If it is a gospel scene, what is it like to look into the eyes of Jesus and to experience his presence? What is he telling me? How do I respond?

The point of these exercises is to enable an encounter with Christ himself through the biblical story—an account that is not just history, but the story of every believer. By engaging in Scripture, we engage Jesus in our own story of life. This deep listening to the biblical text then leads us to respond to what we have experienced, by beginning a spiritual conversation with Jesus within the scene. That conversation, listening and responding, then continues as we learn to discern how God is leading us.

This process of engaging the imagination, the way of Ignatian spirituality, is ultimately so that we can experience God in all things and live for God's glory. The Ignatian way is always concerned with discernment—continually seeking to understand what is the right path to glorify God in our lives. This spiritual way helps us learn how to move away from living for our lower desires, and shows us a way to direct their energies toward the fulfillment of our higher purpose in life.

Seeking Beauty through Scripture

For the masses of Christians through the ages, most of whom

have been illiterate and unable to read the biblical texts, church art and architecture have displayed the biblical story of salvation. Byzantine mosaics display the scenes of Scripture in a wondrous way, and Gothic cathedrals present the Bible in stone and glass. But because we are literate Christians, we know that the Bible itself is also beautiful. In fact, its literature is far more captivating than an ancient basilica. When we search for the beauty in the sacred pages, we can experience the splendor of the word of God.

The Greek philosophers and the church fathers spoke of three prime virtues: truth, goodness, and beauty. As prime virtues, they need no further justification—they are their own justification, which is a way of saying that these virtues don't need to be made practical—they don't have to do anything to be of value. Their value is inherent; we simply choose them because they are true, good, and beautiful. The early theologians located the source of these prime virtues in God. So these virtues become a guide to Christian living as we seek to believe what is true, become what is good, and behold what is beautiful.

We are used to seeking truth in Scripture, and we often interpret the Bible as a guide to goodness. But it is the third virtue, the virtue of beauty, that has been most de-emphasized in the way we understand the Bible. As a result, Christianity has suffered a loss of beauty—a loss that needs to be recovered.

When we seek truth and goodness in Scripture, we realize that this divine truth and goodness is persuasive. But we also need a corresponding emphasis on beauty so that we see that God's word is attractive. Scripture is capable of not only persuading with truth and goodness, but also of attracting with beauty. We need to see the word of God as something beautiful. Sometimes where truth and goodness cannot convince, beauty can entice.

We must learn to be drawn into the Bible like being drawn into a wonderful work of art. The characters and the scenes capture our imaginations and invite us into their world. Through the Holy Spirit alive in the text and within us, the Scriptures breathe God's truth, goodness, and beauty. As God's living word, they captivate us and move us toward God's grace, to share in the divine life. The Bible is not just a collection of sentimental sayings, as it is sometimes presented in the West. Rather, like genuine beauty, it is mysterious, dangerous, fascinating, and awesome. As beauty awakens our spirit and opens us to transcendence, the Bible can bring us into the presence of God.

In creating biblical art, the artist interprets the text in such a way as to produce a beautiful work. It is the artist's spiritual vision and profound meditation on the word of God that produces great art. But all believers can reflect on the text, ponder its meaning, and produce a beautiful life. As art grows within the imagination of the Christian artist in response to Scripture, so saints grow within the womb of the church through their response to God's word. And just as a beautiful work of art can evangelize, our lives can announce the good news by the ways we respond to the beauty we discover in the word of God. As Christian art can be a visual gospel, we too can be God's work of art by reflecting and witnessing to God's saving love.

KEYS FOR UNLOCKING THE DOOR

 A holistic reading of Scripture, engaging with God's word with our whole being, enables us to encounter God in the experience.

The Holy Spirit continually breathes life into the sacred pages of Scripture so that they can form our lives.

God desires us to experience the inspired word as nourishing food. God wants us to chew, savor, digest, and absorb it into our whole being.

The church's most ancient way of reading Scripture, called *lectio divina* in the ancient church, leads us to listen to God in Scripture, leading to an intimate encounter with God.

The more we try to understand biblical texts, struggling with their meaning through the results of biblical scholarship, the better we can experience their transforming potential.

The Spiritual Exercises of St. Ignatius of Loyola encourage readers to read with the imagination, leading to a spiritual conversation: listening, responding, and discerning God's direction.

Through the beauty of Scripture, God attracts us to the divine word and entices us to desire divine life.

❖ ❖ ❖

QUESTIONS FOR REFLECTION AT THE THRESHOLD

● What can I do to better read Scripture with my whole being?

● What experience have I had of reading a particular biblical passage from the inside?

- When have I experienced the Spirit of Truth working within me as I read a passage of Scripture?

- In what ways does Ezekiel's vision of eating the scroll encourage me to experience Scripture more fully?

- How can I learn to read Scripture "with the ear of the heart"? What does this phrase of St. Benedict mean to me?

- Choose a gospel passage to read with the imagination, according to the way of St. Ignatius of Loyola. What was the experience like?

- In what ways can reading the Bible be like being drawn into a beautiful work of art? How does Scripture awaken my spirit and open me to transcendence?

❖ ❖ ❖

PRAYER FOR CROSSING THE THRESHOLD

Author of truth, goodness, and beauty, draw me into your divine word with my whole being. Engage my mind, emotions, imagination, and desires so that I may be attracted to your life and be enticed into your embrace. Let me listen to your word with the ear of my heart, and lead me to chew, savor, and absorb your word into my life.

Crossing the Threshold...

9 From Listening to Responding in Prayer

AS WE LEARN TO LISTEN DEEPLY TO GOD'S WORD IN SCRIPTURE, EXPERIENCING THAT WORD IN WAYS THAT ARE INCREASINGLY MORE PERSONAL, WE ALSO LEARN HOW TO RESPOND TO WHAT WE HAVE HEARD. And the natural response to God's word is prayer. If we truly experience Scripture as God's voice addressing us, then we will of course want to personally respond to the voice we have heard.

Some people think that prayer consists of a human appeal to God, which then awaits God's response—we speak, God answers. But the Scriptures and the tradition of Christian spirituality teach us that the opposite is true. In prayer, God's initiative always comes first. Our own initial step at giving voice to our heart is always a response. Left to ourselves, without God's grace, we would not be able to pray at all. The sin of our humanity has weakened our natural desire to pray, and we tend to hide from God and avoid an intimate presence. But God did not create us this way, and God wants to have a deep personal relationship with every person.

Divine grace is at work within every person, calling us to that mysterious encounter called prayer, giving all people the inclination and desire to reach out to God. In this way, prayer grows out of a person's relationship with God, where God is both the ultimate source of prayer and also the object of prayer.

Prayer is a conversation with God that expresses this relationship. In the Old Testament, the relationship is exemplified by Moses, to whom God spoke "as one speaks to a friend" (Exod 33:11). In the New Testament, Jesus invites everyone into friendship with himself. He was called the "friend of sinners," and the night before his death, he acknowledged his disciples as "friends" (John 15:15). Even more, he taught us that we are God's children, calling us into the intimacy of family life with God. While Jesus calls us his friends, he invites us to call God "Father." It was for this reason that we were made: to know God, to be with God, and to enjoy friendship with God in order to share in the community of love that is the Trinity.

So about what do we speak to God in this conversation we call prayer? About God's self and about ourselves. About joys, sorrows, successes, failures, noble ambitions, and daily worries. When we pray, we get to know God, and in getting to know our God, we get to know ourselves, the meaning of our existence, and the purpose of our lives.

The Prayerful Conversation of *Lectio Divina*

The ancient practice of *lectio divina* grows out of a deepening relationship with God. It establishes a dialogue between the reader of Scripture and God. We listen to God through the text and then respond to God in heartfelt prayer. After listening carefully and reflectively to God's word in Scripture, we naturally reach a point in which we want to respond to the One whose voice we have heard. This personal response to God's word is the moment of prayer, and this prayerful conversation with God is the core of *lectio divina*.

The prayerful response in *lectio divina* is not just any type of prayer. It flows directly from reading and reflecting on Scripture as God's word speaking to us. The biblical vocabulary, images, and sentiments of the biblical text are joined with our own thoughts, needs, and desires to form this kind of responsive prayer. Our personal prayer is enriched through the inspired words of the biblical tradition.

The tone of our prayer will depend on what we have heard God saying to us in Scripture. When the text reminds us of the goodness, truth, or beauty of God and divine actions in our lives, we pray in praise and thanksgiving. When it makes us aware of the wrong we have done or the good we have failed to do, we pray with repentance and seek forgiveness. When the text reminds us of our own needs or the needs of others, we pray in petition or intercession.

In some cases, our prayer may even be a rebellion, a crying lament, or an angry tirade, as we see in the literature of Job, Jeremiah, and some of the psalms. In any case, the key to this kind of prayer is that our response to God flows directly from our listening. This prevents our prayer from becoming routine or repetitive. It is always a fresh prayer spontaneously arising from the heart.

In the Sermon on the Mount, Jesus urged his disciples to pray in the private recesses of their home: "Whenever you pray, go into your room and shut the door and pray to your Father who is in secret" (Matt 6:6). Ancient commentators understood this "inner room" as an image of the human heart, our center and our most personal dwelling. This secret place that God alone can see is the most fruitful place for prayer.

When we discover an ability and desire to pray within our hearts, we know that it is a gift of the Holy Spirit. Paul's letter

to the Romans speaks to the uncertainty we have about our
ability to pray and our fearfulness about praying well:

> *Likewise the Spirit helps us in our weakness; for we*
> *do not know how to pray as we ought, but that very*
> *Spirit intercedes with sighs too deep for words. And*
> *God, who searches the heart, knows what is the mind*
> *of the Spirit, because the Spirit intercedes for the saints*
> *according to the will of God.* [ROM 8:26–27]

We all know our weaknesses when it comes to prayer. Our false
self-sufficiency and need for control can stifle the life, grace,
and gifts of the Holy Spirit within us. But if we let God take
control, the divine Spirit will come into our hearts and pray
within us. God alone can see our hearts and so God receives
our Spirit-guided prayer and gives us all that we need according
to the divine plan for our lives.

Prayer requires our active effort to keep our hearts open to
God's Spirit by preparing the way for his work within us. Our
desire is all important. In fact, St. Augustine said, "The desire
to pray is itself prayer."[1] We discover the gift of prayer when
we recover our desire for God. And we eventually realize that
our desire for God is itself the presence of God's Spirit working within us.

Resting in Contemplative Silence

Reading Scripture focuses on words, and praying in response
to Scripture involves more words. But eventually, in our relationship with God, as in all relationships, the need for more
words fades. After reading, reflecting, and praying in words,
the words become unnecessary after a while and no longer
helpful. They have taken us as far as they can. So we move from
conversation with God to communion with God.

In the practice of *lectio divina*, our prayer with words leads to a prayerful silence, a contemplative presence with God. We simply end our prayer with an effortless resting in God, receiving and accepting the transforming embrace of the One who has revealed the inspired word to us. This contemplative silence requires that we let go of any effort to be in charge of the process. When we feel God drawing us into a deeper awareness of the divine presence, we gradually abandon our intellectual activity and let ourselves be wooed into God's embrace. We no longer have to think or reason, listen or speak.

This wordless presence with God seems rather "useless," from a practical point of view. For this reason, contemplation is more difficult to experience today than in previous ages. In the mind-set of our culture, we define people primarily by their "doing" rather than by their "being." We judge our own life and that of others by successes and achievements. According to this way of thinking, simply being in the presence of God without accomplishing anything seems like a waste of time to many people.

Saints and theologians of earlier centuries considered contemplation as part of the normal experience of prayer for every Christian. Most considered it a higher stage, reached along the road of receptive listening and vocal prayer, but they believed it was a natural phase of prayer available to anyone with an open heart. But because of our contemporary mind-set, the development of contemplation seems far less natural and spontaneous than it was in previous centuries, and people today often exclude contemplation from their prayer.

All the material and technological accomplishments of the twenty-first century are not without their price. Never before in history have people been so prone to analyze, intellectualize, and control everything about life. The analytical faculties of our minds overshadow the intuitive faculties that we need so much for contemplation. Our pragmatic intellects have triumphed over the receptive intuition that brings us into communion with the divine.

If we spend all of our time in extroverted activity, we become strangers to our own inner life. By denying ourselves the environment in which to cultivate contemplation, we deny ourselves a fuller understanding of our true self and the personal transformation made possible through a deeper relationship with God. In contrast to the rapid, noisy communication of our technological world, quiet, receptive stillness is the atmosphere in which the most important communication occurs.

Moments of this kind of wordless presence occur in any loving relationship. The experience resembles that of lovers holding each other in gentle silence or of a sleeping child resting in her mother's arms. These moments make us long for a greater spiritual depth in other aspects of our life. We long for a way to relate to God and others that does not depend on what we do and what we accomplish, but on who we are at the deepest level. This is the kind of presence that contemplative prayer can offer us. Although it might seem passive and useless, we can be assured that God is working deep within us when we humbly expose our heart, the center of our being, to him. We can know that God's grace is truly at work in these moments and that the Holy Spirit is transforming us in gentle ways toward the life that God desires for us.

Learning from the Prayers of Scripture

Prayers of every form and style fill the pages of the Bible, from Genesis to Revelation. Although we usually experience the Bible as God's word to us, a significant part of Scripture is words spoken to God. So the Bible is not just God's revelation to people; it is communication between God and people. All of the great figures of the Bible prayed to God, each of them showing us some distinctive way of addressing the divine. They offer us models for our own prayer and may particularly influence the shape, vocabulary, and spirit of our prayer.[2]

Moses, the one known to speak face-to-face with God, was both an intercessor for the people and a partner with God in the divine plan for Israel. Deborah prayed to God after her victory over Israel's enemies. Hannah prayed for the gift of a child, and then in gratitude for God's gift. The prayers of David are prayers of praise and petition, lament and contrition. Solomon prayed at the dedication of the temple for wisdom and for blessings upon God's people.

The prayers of God's prophets are found scattered throughout their literature. Elijah offered prayers of petition for divine favor. Jeremiah prayed his laments and complaints with unrestrained emotion. Daniel was faithful in prayer even under the most difficult of circumstances.

In Israel, prayer was not limited to prophets, kings, and priests. Prayer was practiced daily by all God's people and could be recited anywhere at any time. It was both public and private, formal and personal, liturgical and spontaneous. Though biblical prayers are sometimes long and extravagant, most are short, simple, and direct. The Bible shows that people prayed while standing, kneeling, lying prostrate on the ground, bowing, or lifting their hands. Their physical position indicates the involvement of the whole person—mind, body, emotions, and will—but what it reflects most is the orientation of the heart in relationship to God.

The Bible shows us that God's people rejected the notion that prayer is magical or an attempt to manipulate God. They did not seek to flatter God or grovel for God's reply, but they trusted that their prayers were heard and that God would respond. They understood that prayer is communication, a natural response to God's self-revelation, marked by intimacy and trust.

The book of Psalms is the only biblical book that consists entirely of prayers. We can find every type of prayer there: prayers of praise, thanksgiving, lament, petition, confidence, confession, and more. The psalmists offered praise for God's great glory and reflected on the wonders of the natural world, God's great deeds among the people, and the joys of human life. They expressed delight in moments of blessing, and they lamented in times of loss, grief, and frustration. They brought the full range of human emotion to prayer: from confidence, happiness, and gratitude, to sorrow, fear, and despair, even anger and rage. This unreserved, fullhearted prayer was Israel's way of affirming God's presence with them and being assured of God's unfailing concern.

Learning to Pray as Jesus Taught Us

Jesus recited the prayers of Israel, especially the psalms, both in the liturgical prayer of his people and in his own personal prayer. These prayers are quoted throughout the gospels, both on the lips of Jesus and in reference to his life. Clearly, Jesus had internalized the psalms and other Jewish prayers, and they arose spontaneously from his lips in times of joy and sorrow.

The church never composed its own book of psalms, but used Israel's "prayer book" as its own. Just as the Jewish people through the centuries used the psalms to pray in situations far different from those in which they were composed, the early Christians used them to express praise, thanksgiving, confidence, and lamentation. And because the psalms were the prayers of Jesus, his followers have prayed them for centuries in his name.

Through these ancient prayers, Jesus teaches us that we can pray with words that are not our own. Reciting words written thousands of years ago, we open our hearts to pray the inspired words of our ancestors. When we are praying a psalm, our feelings don't even need to be in harmony with the emotions the prayer expresses. We open ourselves to encompass the entire body of Christ—praising, thanking, repenting, and lamenting with all of God's people. The psalms give us an opportunity to put the experiences of happiness, gratitude, grief, and anguish felt by others into our own hearts and transform them into prayer. We learn to "rejoice with those who rejoice, weep with those who weep" (Rom 12:15). This inspired collection of prayers endures because of the variety of thoughts and feelings we find there and because the Holy Spirit constantly breathes life into them. After three millennia, they are still the prayers of the people of God.

Jesus taught his followers to pray by his example. The gospels show him habitually in prayer, often going away to pray in solitude. He sought communion with the Father in order to renew his ministry and to find direction at critical moments. We see Jesus in prayer from the beginnings of his public life until his prayer in the Garden of Gethsemane and his final prayer on the cross.

Even though the disciples prayed the psalms and the other prayers of the Jewish tradition with Jesus, there must have been something different about the way that he prayed—something they wanted to share. So, after Jesus had finished praying in a certain place, "one of his disciples said to him, 'Lord, teach us to pray'" (Luke 11:1). It was on this occasion that Jesus taught them what we know as the Lord's Prayer.

The most distinctive characteristic of Jesus' prayer is that he addressed God as "Father." Because the God of Abraham, Isaac, and Jacob was his father, Jesus addressed him with the same familiarity and affection that a son or daughter has with his or her parents. When his disciples asked Jesus to teach them to pray, they were asking to enter into this intimate relationship with the Father. So Jesus taught them to turn to his father as their father, to pray to God as "our Father." Jesus taught them to pray in this way because he was establishing a new relationship between God and his disciples, making them sons and daughters of God.

Through Jesus' saving death and resurrection and the presence of his Spirit within us, we are adopted as children of God, and we can address him as "Abba," Father. And so our prayers, like the Lord's Prayer, can be simple and confident. Prayers worthy of God's attention do not have to be wordy or elaborate. A child can simply ask for basic needs on a daily basis, as well as express gratitude for the good things a parent provides. There is no need to multiply words or create formal, artificial language. Our God knows our hearts and our needs. We can pray to God with assurance and trust.

The Lord's Prayer is inspired Scripture, and we can pray it without hesitation because it comes directly from the heart of Jesus. But it is also a model for all of our prayer. Whenever we pray we can use words that are natural for us, that reveal what is really in our minds and hearts. We can freely express our praise of God when we worship, our sorrow when we are sad, our joy when we are happy, and our apology when we are repentant. Simplicity, directness, honesty, and confidence—these are the qualities of prayer that Jesus teaches us and the marks that characterize the prayer of a disciple.

❖ ❖ ❖

KEYS FOR UNLOCKING THE DOOR

Prayer is our response to God, part of the conversation that expresses our relationship with God.

The prayerful response in *lectio divina* flows from our listening to Scripture and teaches us to pray with richer vocabulary, images, and emotions.

The Holy Spirit gives us the desire and ability to pray because "the Spirit helps us in our weakness; for we do not know how to pray as we ought."

Reading, reflecting, and praying with Scripture leads to the wordless silence of contemplation.

Spiritual writers of the church's early centuries considered contemplation as a normal and natural part of prayer for anyone with an open heart.

All the great figures of the Bible prayed to God, filling the Bible with prayers and showing us a variety of ways of addressing God.

Through his example, Jesus teaches us to pray with simplicity, directness, honesty, and confidence.

❖ ❖ ❖

QUESTIONS FOR REFLECTION AT THE THRESHOLD

- Why do I find prayer difficult, when God desires me to experience divine love?

- What kind of prayers do I pray most often? What can I do to widen the range of my prayer?

- What did St. Augustine mean when he said, "The desire to pray is itself prayer"?

- In what sense is contemplation a natural and normal part of a growing relationship with God?

- What can I learn about prayer from the prayers of God's people throughout the Bible?

- How can I learn to pray the Psalms along with the whole body of Christ in the world?

- In what ways is the Lord's Prayer a model prayer that teaches me how to pray?

❖ ❖ ❖

PRAYER FOR CROSSING THE THRESHOLD

God our Father, send us your Holy Spirit to give us the desire and ability to pray. Expand the words, images, and emotions of my prayer as you deepen my relationship with you.
Teach me to pray as Jesus prayed to you, in words and in silence, in solitude and in public, with simplicity, directness, honesty, and confidence.

Crossing the Threshold...

10 From Word to Worship to Witness

THE DOORWAY TO EXPERIENCING GOD'S WORD IN SCRIPTURE OPENS INWARD AND IT OPENS OUTWARD. It invites us inward to listen, reflect, and pray with Scripture; then it moves us outward to bring God's word into the many places of our lives. Both these inward and outward impulses grow together in the hearts of those who experience Scripture as God's word.

Reading and studying the Bible enriches both our internal and external life. The word of God teaches us, forms our heart, and deepens our spirit. It also helps us see God's presence in our work and family life, moves us to form friendships and community, forms our conscience to do what is right, gives us compassion for the lost, and opens our eyes to the work of justice. Prayerfully listening to Scripture allows us to see the deepest meaning in the issues, problems, and events of our lives and of the world. By savoring God's word within us, we open our lives to become more deeply involved in the transforming process that the word has provoked throughout human history.

From Hearing to Doing God's Word

We all know that if people do what they say they are going to do, their word has integrity. The saying "You're only as good as your word" illustrates the necessary bond between our personal effectiveness and the words we express. A person's word is weighed not only by the ideas it communicates, but by the results it achieves.

God's word not only communicates ideas but also contains the power to create change. As the psalmist says, "By the word of the Lord the heavens were made" (Ps 33:6). That divine word continues to create and is the primary cause of the world's ongoing existence and progress.

So many of the words we hear and speak throughout the day have no effect. But the word that goes forth from the "mouth" of God always achieves its purpose. In a beautiful poetic metaphor, the prophet Isaiah speaks about God's word as a penetrating rain and blanketing snow, giving moisture to the earth so that it may bear fruit:

> For as the rain and the snow come down from heaven
>   and do not return there until they have watered
>   the earth,
> making it bring forth and sprout,
>   giving seed to the sower and bread to the eater,
> so shall my word be that goes out from my mouth;
>   it shall not return to me empty,
> but it shall accomplish that which I purpose,
>   and succeed in the thing for which I sent it.
> {Isaiah 55:10–11}

As the rain and the snow fall to the earth, they meet a yearning receptivity. The ground receives their welcome moisture as an assurance that the seeds will sprout and eventually bear fruit.

Sometimes God's word falls on deaf ears or distracted minds. But if we listen and open our hearts, eventually that word will penetrate the parched soil of our lives. Not only will God's word refresh us and help us to grow, it will cause us to bear the fruit that God intends for us to share.

God desires the divine word to have an effect on us, but it will not unless we allow its power to be activated within us. As James wrote, "Be doers of the word, and not merely hearers" (James 1:22). Though listening is the first step for reading Scripture as God's word, putting that word into action is the culminating result. Through the process of listening, reflecting, praying, and activating God's word, it will achieve its purposes within us and bring forth renewed life.

The power of God's word is not just confined to our hearts. The change it effects in us makes for change in our lives and in the world. Our obedience to the word planted in our hearts makes us channels for God's compassion and mercy. Being a "doer of the word" enables us to act as instruments of God's grace so that God may bring the divine and loving plan to fulfillment.

The Word of God Leads to the Worship of God

When we view biblical mosaics, paintings, and stained glass on the walls of museums, we can certainly appreciate their artistic quality. But when they are incorporated into the churches for which they were created, they express their original purposefulness in glorifying God. Likewise, when we listen to sacred music performed in a concert hall, we can certainly enjoy its uplifting beauty. But when it is integrated into the church's liturgy, it becomes part of the worship of God's people for which it was composed. The same is true with the Bible. We can read Scripture with genuine appreciation as great literature. We can read it also in prayerful and reflective study, and experience it as God's word. But when the Scriptures are read or chanted in the liturgy of the church, the word of the Lord attains its fullest realization.

The tradition of Israel and the church demonstrates the unity of Scripture and liturgy. The gathered community of God's people is the most natural setting for sacred Scripture because, by and large, the texts were written for communal worship. In the liturgy, the sacred texts are proclaimed and "actualized." The Scriptures usher the worshipers into the liturgical action, and the word of God is made alive and effective for the worshipers.[1]

The proclamation of God's word within the assembly has always been an integral part of the praise, thanksgiving, and sacrificial worship of God's people. In the celebration of Israel's Sabbaths and feasts, the Scriptures were proclaimed and chanted in the temple, synagogues, and homes. The covenant with God was periodically renewed by gathering the people, reading from the scrolls of God's revelation preserved in the sanctuary, and offering sacrifice.

Likewise, for the early Christians, the worshiping assembly was the primary place in which God's people heard the Scriptures. In word and sacrament, believers were baptized into Christ and experienced his risen life in Eucharist. And the texts of the New Testament were created, proclaimed, and canonized within the context of the church's liturgy. The apostles wrote letters to be read in the church when the believers gathered on the Lord's Day. Soon after being written, the four gospels began to be proclaimed in the eucharistic liturgy of the church. Both the books of the Old and New Testaments were selected and canonized not so much for private study as for liturgical reading. The list of books that eventually formed the complete Bible were those most fit for use in the church's public worship. The councils of the church essentially ratified the canon of Scripture that was already being read in the worship and sacramental life of the church.

The Mass and all the sacraments of the church are formed from the Scriptures and by the Scriptures. All the parts of the liturgy, the ritual words and the ritual actions, find their origin in the Scriptures of Israel and the apostolic Scriptures of the church. When we consider the form and vocabulary of the introductory rites, the liturgy of the word and of the Eucharist, and the closing rites and blessings, as well as the rituals of each of the church's sacraments, we see that they are all drawn from the Bible.[2]

This unity of Scripture and eucharistic worship is demonstrated in Luke's Emmaus account. We first see that along the journey to Emmaus, the risen Jesus is present with his disciples, opening the Scriptures to them: "Then beginning with Moses and all the prophets, he interpreted to them the things about himself in all the Scriptures" (Luke 24:27). He shows how all the ancient texts come to their completion in him, joining Israel's covenant with his climactic death and resurrection. Then, at table, Jesus becomes known to the disciples in the breaking of the bread. The interrelationship between opening the Scriptures and the breaking of the bread, the liturgy of the word flowing into the liturgy of the Eucharist, has formed the structure of the church's eucharistic liturgy through the ages.

From the Reformation in the sixteenth century until recent decades, Catholic practice has focused on the real presence of Christ's Body and Blood in the eucharistic elements, because of challenges to the church's sacramental teachings. On the other hand, Protestant practice has focused on the Scriptures, to the detriment of the church's liturgical and sacramental tradition. But in the earlier liturgy of the church, the transforming power of Scripture and its authority as God's word received as much emphasis as Christ's sacramental presence. As bread and wine are transformed into Christ's Body and Blood, Scripture is transformed into the living word. Both word and sacrament make Christ present to us; both give spiritual nourishment to God's people.

Origen, writing in the third century, indicates the belief of the early church in both the real presence of Christ in the Eucharist and the transforming power of the inspired Scriptures:

> *You are accustomed to take part in the divine mysteries, so you know how, when you have received the body of the Lord, you reverently exercise every care lest a particle of it fall and lest anything of the consecrated gift perish. You account yourselves guilty, and rightly do you so believe, if any of it be lost through negligence. But if you are so careful to preserve his body, and rightly so, why do you think that there is less guilt to have neglected God's word than to have neglected his body?*[3]

Today the whole church has come a long way in restoring this ancient parallelism between the Scriptures and the Eucharist. In many churches of our day, the Scriptures are enthroned for veneration in a similar way as the sacrament is reserved in the tabernacle. In today's liturgy, we often bring candles and incense to the ambo where the Scriptures are proclaimed, as well as to the altar of sacrifice. The ordained minister bows, crosses himself, and kisses the book—gestures of reverence signifying that Christ is present in the gospels as well as at the sacrament of the altar. When the gospels are proclaimed, worshipers greet the presence of the Lord with the words, "Glory to you, O Lord."

St. Jerome, in the fourth century, reminds us that Scripture is a real encounter with Christ. He exhorts his listeners to satisfy their hungers and quench their thirsts both through eucharistic communion and through the reading of Scripture:

> *Since the Lord's flesh is real food and his blood real*
> *drink...our only good in the present age is to eat his*
> *flesh and drink his blood, not only in the eucharistic*
> *mystery but also in the reading of Scripture.*[4]

This unity of the word of God and the eucharistic presence of Christ is expressed by the dual emphasis of the *Dogmatic Constitution on Divine Revelation*. Both are to be venerated by the faithful, since they each nourish God's people as the bread of life:

> *The church has always venerated the divine Scriptures*
> *just as she venerated the Body of the Lord, in so far as*
> *she never ceases, particularly in the sacred liturgy, to*
> *partake of the bread of life and to offer it to the faithful*
> *from the one table of the word of God and the Body of*
> *Christ.*[5]

Both word and sacrament are necessary for the full expression of Christ's presence with his church. The Mass, we might say, is the Bible in action, the saving truths and events of Scripture made present and real before us in the eucharistic liturgy. A sacrament, as Augustine said, is a *visibile verbum,*[6] "a visible word." The sacramental rite enacts within the believing assembly the deepest sense of the proclaimed word.

What the individual experiences in *lectio divina*, the worshiping assembly experiences in the Mass. The individual receives God's word, meditating on it and assimilating it; then the believer responds to God's word in prayer, contemplation, and deeds. Likewise, in the eucharistic ritual, Christ speaks to his church, and we respond in worship and in action on behalf of the world. In this way, *lectio divina* leads to and flows from the liturgy of the church.

The church's eucharistic liturgy won't let us read our Bible individualistically. We can't just join with our Bible study friends each week and let it go at that. The liturgy brings us into a confrontation with God's word in the company of the people of God throughout time and space—joining us with the angels and saints, and with brothers and sisters throughout the world—listening and responding to God's living word.

Then, after joining us together, the liturgy sends us out, to proclaim with our lives the reality we have experienced. "Go and announce the Gospel of the Lord" and "Go in peace, glorifying the Lord by your life"—these are two of the closing acclamations by which we are sent out from the Mass and into the world. After celebrating the Lord's presence in word and sacrament, we are commissioned to go forth and evangelize.

The Word of God Leads to Witness in the World

The liturgy of the church is marked by two primary movements. First, it brings people from the world into the sanctuary for communal worship, gathering them to listen, believe, and receive. Then, it moves people out of the sanctuary and back into the world. Having encountered Christ in word and sacrament, we travel back to the places where we spend our lives to witness and to serve.

Personal reading of Scripture should follow this same dynamic. First we listen to the word, take it in as living bread, and digest it into our very being. Then, animated by the living word, we metabolize it into good deeds and devoted witness. The sacred page is transformed through us, in the name of Jesus, into cups of cold water for the thirsty, to feet washed in service, to visits to the imprisoned, to food for hungry children, to compassion for the immigrant and the outcast.[7]

The two disciples on the road to Emmaus recalled their experience of listening to the Scriptures with Jesus, and they said, "Were not our hearts burning within us while he was opening the Scriptures to us?" As they heard the inspired words, their hearts began to catch fire. In fact, every passage of Scripture is like a burning ember. It has the potential to spark off the page, spread, and consume. And as we read them, we might just catch fire, letting God's "pentecostal" fire fill our lives.

When we truly experience the living book of inspired Scripture, our lives will change. The faithful reader must become open not only to intelligent understanding of the text but also to personal abduction by its message. The more we remove the obstacles that we put in the way, the more powerfully Scripture can burn in our hearts and transform us. Occasionally the changes are remarkable, as we see in the lives of many of the saints. But more often the transformation happens in gradual ways. We can always discern change within us by measuring our internal life against the fruit of the Spirit: love, joy, peace, patience, kindness, generosity, faithfulness, gentleness, and self-control. As we discern this fruit in the way we live, we then know that the word of God is slowly transforming us from within.

This personal transformation by the word of God leads believers to witness in the world. When we read and pray the Scriptures in this way, our very being becomes a witness to others. When our lives are transformed through Scripture, we cannot help but communicate the good news of Jesus with our very presence. All of our words and actions witness to others what animates our lives.

Through the transforming word of God, we become a new creation living "in Christ." Incorporated into the saving community of the body of Christ, we become part of a community that transcends the boundaries that divide people between Jews and Gentiles, slaves and free people, rich and poor, women and men. Part of the dramatic witness the church offered to first-century society was this attractive, alternative community of dissimilar people called into a higher unity in Christ.

The new life offered to us in Christ is a liberated life. A believer is no longer imprisoned by the prejudices, resentments, and jealousies that so often dominate human life. The church not only includes people of every language, race, and culture, but it also brings them into interdependent relationships. When we extend grace to others and make peace with one another, we become boundary breakers, and, in so doing, we offer a powerful witness of Christ to our world.

The church, when it embodies the life of God's new creation, is always attractive to the world, and people are drawn to it. The church then reflects its primary mission of being the living sign of God's redeemed creation for the sake of his glory. Paul told the young churches that their new life must be evident to all, that they must win the respect of outsiders and shine as stars in the midst of the corrupt and perverse culture of the Roman Empire. The same is true today. Christians, through their unity, exemplary conduct, mutual love, and radiant joy, witness to the world simply by being who they are in Christ. The mission of the early church remains the mission of the church today.

One of the characteristics of many of the books of the Bible, especially the four gospels and the Acts of the Apostles, is their quality of open-endedness. These works leave their readers with the definite sense that the text is incomplete. As we read these books as the word of God, we realize that it is up to us to complete the message, to proclaim Christ's resurrection, to continue to witness the good news to the ends of the earth. The Scriptures convince us that being a disciple of Jesus and a member of his church is not just a static acceptance of Jesus' teachings. It is a dynamic following in Jesus' footsteps, traveling with him along the way, attracting others to this journey, and opening up the horizon of the church to all people.

Open the Door to the Word of God

One of the characteristic images of our culture today is the closed door. Growing fear and insecurity causes people to live behind locked doors, distrusting the stranger who calls on us. The closed and bolted door is also symbolic of people's lives, of people who have stopped confronting reality, dealing with others, meeting challenges, and facing the future. The closed door conveys insecurity, loneliness, and hopelessness.

While the closed door isolates us, stifles us, and paralyzes us, the open door welcomes the light, invites us to engage with life, and welcomes others. The image of the open door conveys confidence, friendship, and freedom. The Scriptures are the story of God opening doors. God is forever calling people to cease fearing, to trust, to live freely, and to hope in the future.

In the Acts of the Apostles, Paul and his companions returned to Antioch after their missionary journey; they recounted all that God had done and "how he had opened a door of faith for the Gentiles" (Acts 14:27). God doesn't want anyone to be excluded. Faith is a grace, but it involves deciding to be with the Lord so as to live with him and to invite others to share in this life. The door of faith is opened for everyone, and all are invited to cross the threshold.

Pick up the Bible, the book of Christ and his church, and pass through the open door. Welcome the risen Lord, the eternal Word, into your life. The first step across the threshold begins a journey that lasts a lifetime. Allow your life to be formed by the inspired word of God, a transforming word that can mold your heart and change your life. Learn to live in Christ, to be a new creation, and to live the kind of life that lasts forever.

❖ ❖ ❖

KEYS FOR UNLOCKING THE DOOR

🔑 God's word not only communicates ideas but it also creates change and bears fruit.

🔑 The Scriptures lead to liturgy, where the word of God is made effective through sacramental worship.

🔑 The sacred books of ancient Israel and the early church were written to be proclaimed in the temple, synagogue, and Christian worship.

🔑 The worship of the early church expressed the transforming power of Christ through unity between word and sacrament.

🔑 The sacramental rite enacts within the believing assembly the deepest sense of the proclaimed word. As Augustine said, a sacrament is "a visible word."

🔑 When our lives are transformed through Scripture, we cannot help but communicate the good news of Jesus through the words and deeds of our witness.

🔑 The open-ended Scriptures invite us to continue the mission that God began in ancient Israel and the early church, opening the doors of salvation to people everywhere.

❖ ❖ ❖

QUESTIONS FOR REFLECTION AT THE THRESHOLD

● What does the instruction of James, "Be doers of the word, and not merely hearers," mean to me?

● What are some of the ways in which the life of ancient Israel demonstrated the unity of Scripture and liturgy?

● What is the primary criterion for selecting certain books to be included in the church's canon of sacred Scripture?

● In what ways does the church today give honor to the nourishing presence of Christ in both the word proclaimed from the ambo and the sacrament offered at the altar?

● In what ways does the experience of an individual in the practice of *lectio divina* parallel the experience of the worshiping assembly in eucharistic worship?

● How do I know that the word of God is having an effect in my life?

● In what ways has the open door and the threshold become an invitation to me through the pages of this books?

❖ ❖ ❖

PRAYER FOR CROSSING THE THRESHOLD

Saving God, throughout the history of salvation you have been opening the doors of faith, inviting people to stop fearing, to trust in you, to live freely, and to hope in the future. Help us to listen to your word and to witness to your word, so that we may be true disciples of Jesus and share the gospel with all.

Endnotes

Chapter 1

1 Adapted from *The Ascent of Mt. Carmel*, 22, 3, in *The Works of St. John of the Cross* (London: Hasell, Watson & Viney, Ltd., 1922).

2 Augustine, *Quaestiones in heptateuchum* 2, 73: *Patrologia Latina* 34, 623.

3 Hugh of St. Victor, *The Ark of Noah*, 2, 8: *Patrologia Latina* 176, 642c.

Chapter 3

1 Jerome, *Commentaries on the Letter to the Galatians* 5, 19-21: *Patrologia Latina* 26, 417a.

Chapter 5

1 N. T. Wright, *The New Testament and the People of God* (Minneapolis: Fortress Press, 1992), p. 143.

Chapter 6

1 Stephen J. Binz, "Contextual and Transformative Interpretation," Anselm Academic Study Bible (Winona, MN: Anselm Academic, 2013), pp. 107-109.

Chapter 7

1 Augustine, *Sermons*, 63: *Patrologia Latina* 38, 424.

Chapter 8

1 Quoted from Eltin Griffin, "Lectio Divina," http://carmelites.ie/lectiodivina.html.

2 Jerome, *Commentaries on Isaiah*, 18, Prologue: *Patrologia Latina* 24, 17b.

3 *Scala Claustralium*, *Sources Chretiennes* 163 (Paris: Cerf, 1942); *The*

Ladder of the Monks and Twelve Meditations by Guigo II (Garden City, NY: Doubleday Image,1978).

4   See Stephen J. Binz, *Conversing with God in Scripture: A Contemporary Approach to Lectio Divina* (Frederick, MD: The Word Among Us Press, 2008).

5   Benedict, *The Rule of Saint Benedict*, Prologue.

6   Ambrose, *Orationes sive meditations*, Prologue.

7   Ambrose, *Commentaries on the Psalms* I, 33: Patrologia Latina 14, 984.

Chapter 9

1   Augustine, *Explanations of the Psalms*, 37, 14: Patrologia Latina 36, 404.

2   See Stephen J. Binz, *Learning to Pray in Scripture* (Huntington, IN: Our Sunday Visitor, 2011).

Chapter 10

1   See Scott Hahn, *Letter and Spirit: From Written Text to Living Word in the Liturgy* (New York: Doubleday, 2005).

2   See Stephen J. Binz, *The Mass in Scripture, The Sacraments in Scripture,* and *The Creed in Scripture* (Huntington, IN: Our Sunday Visitor, 2012).

3   Origen, *On Exodus*, 13.3.

4   Jerome, *Commentary on Ecclesiastes*, 3: Patrologia Latina 23, 1039a.

5   *Dei Verbum*, 21; *CCC*, 103.

6   Augustine, *Tractatus in evangelium Iohannis*, 80, 3.

7   See Stephen J. Binz, *Scripture—God's Handbook for Evangelizing Catholics* (Huntington, IN: Our Sunday Visitor, 2014).

THRESHOLD BIBLE STUDY

THRESHOLD BIBLE STUDY is a dynamic, informative, and inspiring way to learn about Scripture. Each of these 30-lesson, theme-based books will help you to explore new dimensions of your faith, discover deeper insights for your life, and open the door of your heart to the risen Christ. Great for personal reflection as well as group study.

Advent Light

Angels of God

Eucharist

The Feasts of Judaism

The Holy Spirit
and Spiritual Gifts

Jerusalem, the Holy City

Mysteries of the Rosary

The Names of Jesus

People of the Passion

Pilgrimage in the
Footsteps of Jesus

The Resurrection
and the Life

The Sacred Heart of Jesus

Stewardship of the Earth

The Tragic and
Triumphant Cross

Jesus, the Messianic
King (Part 1):
Matthew 1–16

Jesus, the Messianic
King (Part 2):
Matthew 17–28

Jesus, the Word
Made Flesh (Part 1):
John 1–10

Jesus, the Word
Made Flesh (Part 2):
John 11–21

Jesus, the Suffering
Servant (Part 1):
Mark 1–8

Jesus, the Suffering
Servant (Part 2):
Mark 9–16

Jesus, the
Compassionate Savior
(Part 1): *Luke 1–11*

Jesus, the
Compassionate Savior
(Part 2): *Luke 12–24*

Church of the Holy
Spirit (Part 1): *Acts of
the Apostles 1-14*

Church of the Holy
Spirit (Part 2): *Acts of
the Apostles 15-28*

The Lamb and the
Beasts: *The Book
of Revelation*

For a description of each study, visit our
website at **www.ThresholdBibleStudy.com**
or call us at **1-800-321-0411**